Dollar

Col. Wm. C. Hunter

Alpha Editions

This edition published in 2021

ISBN : 9789355112811

Design and Setting By
Alpha Editions
www.alphaedis.com
Email - info@alphaedis.com

Contents

Groundwork	- 1 -
Learn to Say No.	- 3 -
Credit	- 5 -
Never Quit Work	- 8 -
Stand When Selling	- 10 -
The Best Vantage Ground	- 11 -
Ambition	- 12 -
Lawyers	- 13 -
Be a Producer	- 15 -
The Man—Not the Plan	- 18 -
Compensation	- 20 -
Sizing Up Things	- 23 -
Competition	- 26 -
Advertising	- 28 -
Buying	- 30 -
Expenses	- 31 -
Advice	- 35 -
Reading	- 36 -
Argument	- 38 -
Speculation	- 39 -
Elimination	- 42 -

The Specialist - 43 -
The String - 45 -
Horse Sense - 46 -
The Manager - 47 -
Selling - 49 -
Vacations - 52 -
Health - 54 -
Patience - 55 -
Hard Times - 57 -
Sleep - 58 -
Grumbling - 59 -
Associates - 60 -
Fixed Charges - 62 -
Cigarets - 64 -
Return Good For Evil - 65 -
Learn to Play - 66 -
Good Fellowship - 67 -
Hard Work - 69 -
Kindness - 70 -
The Salesman - 72 -
Honesty - 74 -
Success - 75 -
Thinking - 77 -
Home Life - 79 -

Optimism	- 80 -
Memory	- 82 -
Worry	- 84 -
Promises	- 87 -
Independence	- 88 -
Short Letters	- 90 -
Perspiration	- 91 -
Friends	- 92 -
Employes	- 94 -
Laxity	- 97 -
Enthusiasm	- 98 -
Catching Up	- 99 -
Anger	- 101 -
Precedent	- 102 -
Financing	- 103 -
Discontent	- 105 -
The Generalist	- 106 -
Our Aches and Pains	- 107 -
Dressing	- 108 -
Declare Monthly Dividends	- 109 -
Debt	- 110 -
Brains—Birth—Boodle	- 112 -
Backbone and Wishbone	- 115 -
Do Good	- 116 -

The Get-Away - 117 -

Double Equipment - 118 -

Initiative - 119 -

Night Work - 120 -

Obedience - 122 -

Pay Day - 124 -

Saving - 125 -

Waiting For Success - 126 -

Our Sons - 127 -

Pull - 129 -

Gossip - 130 -

Bribes - 131 -

Stenographers - 132 -

Hypochondriacs - 133 -

Politics - 134 -

Profanity - 135 -

System - 136 -

Rule of Gold - 137 -

Groundwork

When you cut a melon, your friends will come with eager mouths and sit under your shade tree and help you eat it. Few of these friends would respond to your call for help when you were working in the hot sun raising that melon.

Many people accept the dividends and benefits of friendship but give you a cold shoulder when called upon for assessments of friendship.

The world is full of young men whose objective is snaps. They are looking all the time for what they can get and not what they can give.

To forge ahead, you must give value received. You can't draw out all the time.

The employe must do what he is paid to do and "then some," for it is this "then some" or plus that gets your salary raised.

The employer and employe must realize that each must make profit. It is because there are so many ingrates and so many four flushers that so few succeed.

This book will be welcomed by those who are square, ambitious and patient. It is not theory. It is not preaching. These chapters will be old friends to you, and you may read a few minutes or a few hours. You may read and re-read as often as you wish, for you will always find some new truth impressed on you every time you read.

Keep this book, carry it with you, and you will be benefitted.

Worry and fear will fade and peace and courage will grow within you the more you study these pages.

The writer has "been at it" for 32 years. He has had successes, failures, joys, sorrows, and experienced the passions, the problems, the difficulties you have experienced.

Since the age of ten years he has been upon his own resources and the 32 years since then have been years of study, working and playing, all blended into a happy life.

The jolts, set backs, sorrows, worries, fears and discouragements are the things which made him strong. They were experiences.

Smooth sailing doesn't bring out the stuff one is made of. It takes shadows to make sunlight appreciated.

It takes reverses to make success. It takes hard knocks to polish you. This is a book of experiences, not one of theories.

There is no attempt to make this a literary effort. All the writer hopes for or cares to do is to truthfully state facts and experiences in plain language. Study the thought rather than the expression.

It is Sense the writer wants to express rather than nonsense.

The writer is happy to say that the previous editions sold rapidly and his friends not only read, but pass the word along.

The way to get happiness is to make others happy and the present of one of these books to a friend or employe is a quick way to get happiness.

Let us go along together and consider some of the problems which we all have to face in our business as well as our social life. A volume could be written on each chapter. But volumes are tiresome and herein you will find net values which are the result of boiling down.

So now we have the groundwork of this book. We understand each other. Simply take these truths for their evident worth. You won't agree with the writer in all things, of course not. If, however, you get one truth that will help you, then you have been repaid for reading this book and the writer has been repaid for writing it.

Learn to Say No.

Look over the history of the thousands who have failed in business, and you will find in nearly every instance the failure was due to an inability to say No.

People come to us under various guises and ask us to do things which in our better judgment we had rather not do, and too many have not the backbone to say No.

We are led to invest in mining stocks and to embark in precarious enterprises because we cannot say No.

We endorse notes and go security for our friends, not because we want to but because we cannot say No.

There is a class of "good fellows" who are after us to join them in physical pleasures, the foregoing of which would be better for us physically, financially and mentally. Too many join them because they cannot say No.

It is rarely a man goes off deliberately and gets drunk. The lone drunk is usually the result of sorrow, sudden financial blow or a hard jolt of some sort.

The man who gets drunk generally does so because he cannot say No when bibulous friends press him to take a drink.

The ability to say No, to refrain from going with the crowd, to decline to go down stream is, more than any other one thing in this life, the mark of a strong character.

The one who can say No is going to succeed. Temporarily he may feel ashamed; he may find it hard to withstand the jibes and jeers and criticism of his friends for refusing to join them in things he should not do.

Our old friend—the law of compensation—comes in here, for in proportion as a man has the ability to say No, who has the courage of his convictions, whose duty is to his body and his family before the temptations that surround him, so in proportion as there are few such individuals these individuals stand out as marked successes.

The manager of one of the biggest breweries in the United States has not tasted liquor of any kind in the last twenty years. Surely this man shows his courage, for his action in face of his occupation is a supreme test of backbone and ability to say No.

The embezzler does not start out to do wrong. Some friends want to borrow money or someone needs financial aid temporarily, and, either at the request of friends or because the individual has something he wishes to purchase and has not the patience to wait, he borrows from the firm by means of "the ticket in the drawer" plan. He repeats the operation frequently until his conscience is dulled, and he gets the habit. Some day he wakes up to find he has several tickets in the drawer, and resorts to extreme measures, trying to beat the races, or to win money by gambling on stocks or grain.

One day he finds he is in a dickens of a fix. He sees no way out of it. He takes more money and skips out, only to be caught later on and made to suffer, and all this because he could not say No to temptation.

Learn to say No. Set your jaws firmly and say No. The friends who go back on you and criticize you for saying No to the things that are hurtful to you are unworthy of the name of friends, and you can very well get along without them.

Friends who ask you to do the things you should not do are the very ones who are of no service to you in time of need.

The individual who says No regardless of the flings and taunts that are cast at him is the one who eventually makes a success.

Character counts above all things in the business world. The banker extends credit on character oftener than we imagine. The banker knows how to say No.

A man's credit and character are most important factors in business, and many a man without security has attained magnificent success through untiring energy, ability, character and courage enough to say No.

In proportion as you grow strong and unhesitating in saying No, the temptations and opportunities to say Yes will lessen in number.

Exercise your back bone and your jaw bone, so you can say No and stick to it.

Credit

No factor is so necessary in building up business as credit, and no factor is so necessary in building up credit as truth.

It is comparatively easy to start credit, but the art is to keep credit.

The young business man who says "I want no credit, I buy and sell for cash" makes a mistake. It is all right to pay promptly, but do not establish a spot cash payment basis, for later on, when you ask credit, your creditors will think something is wrong.

Establish a credit whether you need it or not. It is a good advertisement and a frequent help.

Be reasonably slow in paying your bills, but positively sure that you do pay them.

When you get a sharp or blunt letter asking for a settlement, go to your creditor face to face, set a date when you will make a payment and keep your agreement.

Don't be specific as to amount unless you are decidedly sure you can do it. Be specific as to date, however, and be there or have your check there on the date.

Suppose a man owes you $100 and you ask him for it and he says "Here are ten dollars on account, and on next Thursday I will make another payment, and as often as I can I will pay something until you are fully paid up." You don't get angry at that man when you see his intentions are good and he is doing his best.

So long as your creditor gets something every time he writes it keeps him good natured.

It is the man who breaks promises who gets hard usage from the creditors.

If you owe more than your present cash balance can liquidate, make a pro rata payment all around among your creditors. Write a good square letter saying nothing would please you more than to send a check in full, and that this payment is made as evidence of your willingness and intention to keep good faith.

Keep in touch personally with your creditors as far as possible. Talk to them of your plans and prospects. Always tell the truth. Have your account as a moral risk rather than as a Dun or Bradstreet risk.

There is sentiment in business. Creditors have hearts and they have good impulses. They appreciate friendship and especially gratitude. Don't believe a word of that great untruth "There is no sentiment in business."

Don't get angry when asked for money. Admit your slowness and tell your creditor that as an offset for your present slowness you have a good memory and a heart that appreciates, and some day your purchases will be much larger, and those who are your friends now will certainly get the benefit when the time comes that you do not require favors.

An honest, frank, heart to heart talk is most valuable. The credit man keeps the truthful man in mind and his account under his protecting wing. The credit man glories with you, and has a distinct interest in your success when it comes.

It often happens that the small bank or small manufacturer is the best place for the beginner to go for credit. You can get closer to the small growing creditor than you can to the big fellow who is independent.

The big bank is cold blooded. It insists upon security and collateral. Your account in a big bank is only an incidental detail, and the cashier is cold and distant and blunt.

The small bank, however, gives you more time and attention, is more interested in you and can remember you much better than the big bank.

Avoid bad associates. You can't play the races and give wine dinners and maintain strong confidence with your creditors.

You must be worthy of the confidence reposed in you. It is your duty and part of the contract to be reliable and truthful.

Every time a creditor gets out of sorts go to him and pay him something, and he will quiet down.

Be grateful. Don't be afraid to express yourself freely and frequently on this point.

When you are caught up and financially strong stick to those who stuck by you.

Remember, credit is based on confidence in the individual rather than in his bank account.

Don't get into nasty arguments or disputes. Give and take. Be fair. Be square. Keep your temper. Stoop to conquer. Cut out all thoughts of revenge.

When a house does not treat you right, curb your temper, and, as soon as you can, get in touch with some other good house. Tell the new house frankly why you changed.

Credit is a subsidy, and it stands the hustling business man in good stead.

Many men have started in business with a capital only of ability, hard work, honesty and good reputation.

The use or abuse of credit determines whether a man will rise or fall.

Keep your record clean, and if later you get on the shoals your past will stand you in good stead.

If you have been given to sharp practice or dishonesty, woe be unto you when you fall.

Remember these things carefully. Keep in personal touch with your creditors, keep your promises, pay on account when you cannot pay in full, hustle, be honest, keep good company, don't gamble, don't be a sport. If you practice these virtues, offers of aid will come to you rather than flee from you.

Never Quit Work

The average young man makes up his mind that at fifty or sixty years of age he will retire and take things easy for the rest of his days. The average young man makes a great mistake. It is far better to wear out than to rust out.

To the young man work is a drudge, a necessity to keep him alive. In middle age work is an accepted thing and we are used to it, and feel rather the better for having occupation.

In old age work is a necessity to keep the mind and body young.

There is scarcely a more miserable spectacle than the man of fifty or sixty who has retired with ample fortune. He loafs around the house. Goes from one club to another. Gets lonely. Feels blue.

He tries to kill time in the day looking forward to the meeting of his cronies in the evening. The cronies are busy in the day time and they have engagements and pleasures in the evening, so that our retired friend seems to be in the way.

He finds that the anticipation of retirement was a pleasure, and that the realization is a keen disappointment.

"There is nothing," says Carnegie, "absolutely nothing in money beyond a competence."

When one has enough money to buy things for the home, for his family comfort and enjoyment, when he has sufficient income to take care of himself and his family, surplus dollars do not mean much.

The business man should prepare for his future so that if ill health overtakes him he may have the where-with to surround himself with comforts, travel and the best of care.

The man who enjoys pleasures of the home and friends, who trains up young blood to take hold of the business, who travels and enjoys himself as he goes along has the right idea.

We must learn to enjoy life now instead of waiting for tomorrow, for tomorrow may never come.

The man who cashes in, puts his money in bonds and retires from all work goes down hill quickly, and feels he is of no use in the world.

The farmer who moves in town to live on his income is a sorry individual unless he has a garden and chickens, or buys and sells farms, or occupies his time with work of some kind.

The retired, non-working farmer who has moved to town gets up in the morning, goes to see the train come in, whittles a stick, loafs at the hotel or store, goes to the next train, talks of his rheumatism, goes to bed at eight o'clock, and the next day goes through the same rigmarole.

We have all seen these old codgers who have retired. They are not happy because they have quit their life's habit of work, and are rusting out.

Occupation is the plan of nature to keep man happy, so when you have all the money you need, have some occupation or hobby to occupy your time.

The man who retires from any active work is merely counting the days until he dies.

When old age comes and your body or brain won't let you do or care for as much as you could in your younger days, then get lighter work or lighter cares.

Keep busy if it is only raising chickens or gardening, or studying astronomy or botany.

Keep at it as long as you can. Die in the harness instead of fading slowly away.

Cultivate the reading habit in your younger days that it may be a pleasant occupation when your legs and hands grow feeble with age.

When you quit work or occupation of some sort then life has no beauty for you.

Stand When Selling

You can make your point clearer, you can talk with more force, you can impress and convince your customer better if you stand while he is seated.

Have you ever noticed that when you are seated and the other fellow is standing it puts you at a disadvantage? Try it some time.

Have you not noticed that if you are seated and your adversary is standing, when you get enthusiastic and wish to combat his argument, it is impossible for you to get in your best licks while you are seated? You involuntarily rise when you make your strong points and are full of your subject.

How far would a life insurance man or an advertising man get if he sat down and leaned back and relaxed while talking to you?

You will observe that the good solicitor declines with thanks your proffered chair. He stands up, he knows the value of standing.

By the relation between his standing and you sitting it makes him a positive and you a negative force. He forces—you receive.

How much would an orator impress his audience if he delivered his lecture in a sitting posture?

You cannot combat argument very well if you are sitting, nor can you convince others as well sitting as standing.

When you call on a customer carry a busy air with you. Stand up. Talk straight from the shoulder. Make your point and claims clear. Place your position or proposition definitely, forcefully and quickly before your customer. Make a good get-away when you have accomplished your purpose.

If you don't land him the first time, get away anyway. Let him see that your time is money, and that you appreciate that his time is money, too.

Don't visit. Gracefully and politely decline the chair that is offered; say that your limit of time and disinclination to trespass require your stay to be brief.

Stand. Keep busy and active. Get away quickly, and you will be welcome next time.

The short stayer is a welcome guest. He may not land his customers as quickly, but in the end he will land more customers, and hold them closer and retain them longer than the tedious, visiting, social bore who sits and sits and sits.

The Best Vantage Ground

In closing a contract or settling a dispute it makes considerable difference whether you are in the other fellow's office or in your own.

The man in whose office the transaction takes place has the decided advantage.

If you have a disputed bill, or if you wish to make a contract for material or merchandise use every effort to get the other man in your office. When you go to another office you are on the aggressive, when another man comes to your office you are on the defensive.

It is great diplomacy to get the man you deal with to come to you instead of going to him. In proportion as you are diplomatic you will be able to benefit.

If you meet the other man in a club, hotel or a place outside of your office or the other man's office, then the vantage ground is even and neither has the best of it so far as location is concerned.

Starting from an even vantage ground the advantage shifts greatly one way or the other according to whether you go or the other man comes.

Railroad officials, bankers and great merchants realize the importance of having the vantage ground in their favor.

The merchant, for instance, has private rooms and regular office hours for his buyers, and he lets the manufacturers come to him.

Stop a moment and look over your own experience, and you will recall numerous instances where it has been to your advantage to close a deal in your own office.

There is nothing in what we have written in this series of talks that has less theory in it than this particular chapter.

There is no point we have made more surely proven by experience.

The army that attacks the enemy in the enemy's country has the odds against it, as all wars have proven. Men fight best at home on their own vantage ground.

Whether you are buying or selling try to close the deal in your own place of business.

If you have travelers on the road let it be part of their business and duty to invite and persuade customers to call at your place of business when they are in town.

Ambition

A man without ambition had better content himself with learning a trade. A good mechanic is fairly sure of three dollars a day, and fifty-two weeks' employment in the year.

The mechanic does not have many worries. He does not have notes to meet at the bank. He does not have to face the ingratitude of employes and petty jealousies, for he has no employes working for him.

He lays down his tools when the bell rings and goes home to his family. His ambition is to have a good place to sleep, plenty to eat, money enough to buy clothing for his family and to send his children to school, and extra spending money enough over his fixed charges to allow him to take his family to the circus when it comes to town.

Ambition makes men strive to get ahead. Ambition cultivates taking chances.

Nearly every man is a gambler. Some of you will be shocked at this statement, yet upon careful analysis nearly every move a successful business man makes is a gamble. He is betting that he will take in more money than he lays out on a new plan. The man with ambition is a gambler. The man who learns a trade and does not strive to increase his earnings is not a gambler.

We pride ourselves on our ability to buy cheaply, because the cheaper we can buy the greater our earnings will be and the less our gamble.

Any man with two hands and ordinary health can earn a livelihood, but the ambitious man wants to make a name for himself and to make a success in business, so he works harder than he would do if his problem were only the obtaining of money enough to buy the things necessary for his existence.

The moment a man loses ambition, his progress, so far as business advancement is concerned, ceases.

Nearly every successful business today is successful because the proprietors, in the infancy of the business, were filled with ambition which made them work hard.

We are all familiar with the successful business man who loses his ambition. It is an absolute certainty that as soon as a man loses ambition his business falls off, unless he makes it an object to take care of the ambitious young men in his employ, so that they may keep up the pace of progress he established.

Lawyers

Keep in touch with a lawyer, but don't take his advice on business matters.

A lawyer should be like a dictionary—a place of reference.

Lawyers by the very nature of their vocation have much to do with concerns who are in trouble, and with firms who are poorly managed.

Lawyers know law first and business second; the business man knows business first and law second.

The advice of one successful business man is worth the advice of twenty-three lawyers on a matter of business.

Use the lawyer to keep you out of trouble. Let him see your contracts and the papers and agreements pertaining to leases, sales, purchases, royalties, and all documents which may from their nature be brought into court as evidence. These things are the ones on which to take the lawyer's advice.

When you are pushed into a corner and must fight, then get the best lawyer, for in a fight in court, like a fight in the prize ring, the best trained and equipped man usually wins.

It's more often the best lawyer wins than the best side of the case.

Legal struggles seldom pay. Law suits take up time and money, and the result, even if in your favor, seldom offsets the time, money and worry you have expended.

The good lawyer keeps you from fighting. Many lawyers, however, are grafters, and they advise fight, for they win whether you do or not.

Settle disputes even if you are imposed on. There is little satisfaction in getting a judgment for one hundred dollars, when your lawyers fees are fifty dollars and you have expended two hundred dollars' worth of time and worry over the case.

Ask your lawyer's advice on the legal status of your operations, and not on business propositions.

If you are a success in business that is an evidence, generally speaking, that your judgment is good.

You can get all the advice you want for nothing. If you state a case and lay out a proposed plan, and then ask your friends' advice on the subject, you can safely count that nine out of ten will say that your proposition is all right as outlined by you.

These friends figure that you have given the plan much thought and study, and it is much simpler for them to coincide with your opinion than to take an opposite view.

Honestly between ourselves we must admit that when we seek advice we generally do it only for the purpose of having our own opinions confirmed, and, if our friends do not agree with us, we say they are prejudiced.

Lawyers don't see the smooth, systematic, well balanced side of business, and their knowledge is all negative instead of positive on business matters.

If you have an important move in mind, map out the plan carefully, lay the plan out in detail, be conservative in your estimate of prospective profits, and always make a liberal allowance for cost over the figures you have prepared, and deduct a liberal percentage from the receipts you anticipate. Be very conservative in matters of figures, and then some.

The building you propose to put up will cost far more than your architect tells you. You know this in advance, and you make an allowance for extras, but when the bills all come in you will find that in addition to the estimated cost and the extras which you have figured on, there will be something else to pay.

The sales of a business you propose to embark in will be less than you or your manager figure they will be.

Always allow for enthusiasm and imagination in the matter of prospective receipts.

When your plans are all in shape show the documents, contracts and agreements to your lawyer, and get his legal, but not his personal, advice.

You must be the doctor of your own business.

Remember, a lawyer knows law, and a business man knows business.

Be a Producer

Employes are divided into two classes—the kind that makes profits and the kind that is on the expense side of the ledger.

The young man who has the foresight and ability to get on the selling side, the side that brings profit to the house, has the decided advantage over the young man who is on the expense side.

Book-keepers, stock-keepers, clerks and all other expense employes are paid far lower salaries than the salesmen and buyers, those who produce results.

In the newspaper business the editor with his college education has practically attained his limit of progress when he is 40 years old. He may get from $20.00 to $80.00 or even $100.00 a week as editor.

The young man in the advertising department may get from $50.00 to $200.00 a week. He is a producer of tangible results; the editor produces theoretical results.

In every business the man who sells things, who brings in the profits, is the man who gets the best pay.

The boss will grudgingly give a dollar a week increase to the book-keeper. He only thinks what it would cost him to replace the book-keeper.

The producer gets his increases in $5.00 and $10.00 a week jumps.

The expense employe is in competition with the great army of the unemployed, and there are multitudes who will work for less money than the man who is holding his job on the expense side.

The producer, on the other hand, knows how much profit he is bringing into his house, and if those profits are steadily increasing he may be sure his salary will increase proportionately. If it does not he can always get another position by laying the facts and figures before some more enterprising house.

The producer is seldom out of a situation. If for any reason he is out of employment temporarily he can go to a good house and work on commission, or get a small drawing account, and at three or six months talk salary on actual showing made.

The shrewd business man won't let profits slip away if he can help it, so the real producer sits in a pretty good seat. He has only to show what he can do and he will be paid accordingly.

The expense man's only stock in trade is faithfulness, neatness and amount of detail he can handle. He has little lee-way in the matter of salary, for thousands are faithful, thousands are neat and thousands can perform great amounts of detail.

The young man just out of school should have for his ideal that he shall be a producer first and a proprietor later on. To this end he should equip himself by spending four or five years acquainting himself thoroughly with all the phases and departments of the business and learning the facts about the manufacture of the goods he expects to sell eventually. All this understanding and preparation will be of great service when he is a salesman, and greater service when he is a proprietor.

The writer started wholly dependent upon his own exertions for a livelihood at fourteen years of age. At fifteen he learned shorthand by evening study. At sixteen he attended to the correspondence and mail order department for his employer. At eighteen he was getting $8.00 a week in cash for his services, and many times that amount in valued experience.

"One day he got a blank application for a $75.00 clerkship in the Post Office. At that time appointments were made by political pull and not through the civil service. The writer took the blank to a relative, who was the leading politician of the State. He asked for the endorsement of this senator and received this advice: "Young man, my signature to this sheet would get you the job, but if you were my son I would not let you take the place. I will give you some advice, which is this—never take a political, railroad or bank job. In all these callings you are in competition with thousands of others. The compensation is small, the chance to better your position is remote, and you are a machine. If you want to make a success of life be a producer, learn to sell things."

This advice was acted on, and the writer remembers it as the turning point in his career.

It is a sad thing to see the old man working for $40.00 or $50.00 a month who in the past drew $3,000 or $4,000 a year. Such men were expense men and not producers.

Moves on the checker board of business are made quickly. The man with silver hair may be an accountant or confidential man drawing a good salary. Something happens, his firm goes out of business or sells out, and our old friend is left without a position. He has been used to the comforts and associations a good salary allows, and now he finds himself out of a place and faces the necessity of starting over again, and his competitors are young and active men ready for the battle of life.

The old man out of a job goes around amongst his friends. The friend can do nothing but gives him a letter of recommendation. He is passed along from one to another until he is foot-sore and heart sick and weary of it all.

He winds up as a sleeping car conductor, or gets a position as floor walker or clerk at the inquiry desk.

The producer, be he ever so old or ever so often out of a job, can catch on again. He gets his job on results and not sympathy.

Business men are on the lookout for producers.

Young man, learn to be a producer.

The Man—Not the Plan

We are prone to give credit to the plan as being the thing that makes a successful business. It is not the plan, it is the man behind the plan that is responsible for the success.

The man who has a well-defined ideal, who hews to the line, who eliminates all deterrent influences, who concentrates his energy on his ideal, who bends his efforts towards the one thing is pretty sure to accomplish his purpose.

We often see a man make a marked success in a field that others have considered barren.

Take a small town, for instance, where there are many retail stores. The people of the town will tell the prospective merchant that the town is already overcrowded with stores, that none of the stores seem to be making more than a bare living, and that it would be impossible for another store to make a success, on account of the already overcrowded conditions, yet the right man comes along and starts a store in that town and makes a marked success.

If the plan were the making of success, all an enterprising business man would have to do would be to pick out some plan which was successful and then imitate it.

The great ocean of business has many derelicts on it as a result of copying plans. It is a part of the law of compensation that the man who originates a plan and carries it to successful conclusion has a patent on his business. This patent is his individuality and good business equipment. The man who steals his plan physically is unable to steal the mental end.

Since men have recorded facts in the shape of history, we find that men have made successes of plans and businesses that have been discarded by their predecessors as played-out plans.

When a plan is presented to you do not calculate the outcome by the plan, but by the man.

Two banks may start side by side with exactly the same office furniture and exactly the same business operations. They use the same kind of money; they make loans on lands or on securities. The operations of these two banks may be as closely identical as possible, yet within ten years one bank will have considerable surplus and the other may be out of business.

If the plan were the measure of success these two banks should fare equally well, but the fact that they differed so materially is in itself evidence that the success is determined by the individuals and not the plan.

The illustration of a bank may be carried into other lines, merchandising, manufacturing or railroading.

Compensation

The law of Compensation is—you pay for what you get, or you get what you pay for.

This law says if a horse can run fast it can't pull a good load and vice versa.

This law says a horse cannot go fast far.

It says that for every sorrow there is a joy, for every positive there is a negative.

Where evil exists there is some good to offset it, says compensation.

The law of compensation is the measure optimists use, and in nearly every chapter we have written in this series, compensation will be found as a ground-work.

You can't get away from nor violate this rule of compensation.

It is not new, it is as old as creation itself.

Centuries ago it was expressed this way: "Whatsoever a man soweth that shall he also reap."

Too many try to ignore this great rule, they try to get something for nothing.

You may eat first and pay afterwards, or you may pay first and eat afterwards.

You may play the butterfly; sip life's sweets and sow your wild oats now, but pay day will come and may be you will be unable to pay.

You may spend your income now and suffer want later on.

You may work hard now and play as you go along. You may have happiness each day you live; you can make life worth living if you work.

Happiness is compensation for work; no work, no happiness.

You may have what you want, but, you must pay for it.

Millions cost happiness and often cost health too.

The dinner is properly balanced when it has sweets as well as substantials. The sensible person finds the dinner is better if the sweets come after the substantials.

To violate the law of compensation is to eat the sweets first and then the substantials, and by this law the substantials do not taste good when they are eaten after the sweets.

The man who procrastinates is violating the law of compensation. When you see your duty attend to it at once.

The Boss

By the boss we mean the active proprietor, the executive head, the owner of the business. He is sometimes called the "old man."

The success of an institution depends largely upon the example set by the boss.

If the boss is careless in little things, if he is sharp in his practice, if he does mean acts, he may rely upon it his employes will copy him, and later on, when some blow strikes the business, he will find it has happened through the practices of the employes who got their cues from the boss.

Kindness wins kindness; love wins love. If the boss is generous and charitable, if he sets a good example, he will have an esprit de corps among his employes that is of incalculable value.

There is not one chance in a thousand for the boss to make a success unless he has risen to the position of boss, and climbed and earned his position through steady progress.

The boss must know how to do the things he hires others to do.

The boss who can show an employe his error in a kindly manner and point out a better method, leaves a good feeling in the heart of that employe.

The boss who shows his heart to the employe and is concerned in the things not necessarily business will be repaid a thousand-fold in loyalty and willingness on the part of the employe.

Employes deeply appreciate consideration, and especially the little kindnesses which are not what might be called business practice.

The boss should not be too far aloof; he should be just head and shoulders above those working under him; he should be just far enough above that he stands out as a commander.

He should be willing to grant an audience to an employe and should work with him.

The boss should say we rather than I. He should talk with the employes and not down to them. He should make each individual under him feel that he is part of the institution and an element in its success.

Remember this—employes watch the boss and they copy him. Where you find hard working employes you will find a hard working boss.

The boss cannot run the whole business himself; he is dependent upon willing hands, and, in order to get willing hands, he must have willing hands himself.

If the boss is alert and discovers wastes and leaks in his business, the employes will discover them too, and the business will receive double benefit.

Sizing Up Things

One of the most necessary as well as beneficial practices a man can have is to take fifteen minutes to an hour each day and devote the time to sizing up things, to planning the day's work for the morrow, to threshing the wheat from the chaff, to reviewing the accomplishments of the day.

Sizing up things can only be well done in solitude.

The benefits of sizing up things in solitude are so great it is a wonder more has not been written on the subject.

Plants grow in darkness, yet the common understanding is they grow in sunshine. The sunshine is absolutely necessary for the growth of the plant, but the real growth is done in the quiet darkness.

A man's brain develops in solitude, yet bustle and crowds and business activity are as necessary to the man as sunshine is to the plant.

The real brain and moral growth takes place in solitude.

Here again we must remember the law of compensation, for if a plant had all sunshine and no shadow, and if a man had all hustle and bustle and no solitude, it would be like a machine without a governor; the man and the plant would run so fast something would have to give way.

On the other hand compensation says that if a man is too much in solitude, or the plant too much in darkness, they will wither and die.

Man has always had strong admiration for the strong individual, whether bird, beast, fish, plant or human.

There are two kinds of birds, the kind that lives in flocks, like the blackbird and the wild duck, and the kind that lives by itself, like the eagle. Amongst birds the eagle is chosen as an emblem for the flag, and never the duck or blackbird.

Amongst beasts there are two classes, the herd kind like sheep, and the strong individual, like the lion. The lion is the symbol of strength and courage, the sheep the symbol of innocence and simplicity. The lion appears on coat of arms but not the sheep.

In the fish family there are two classes, the kind that lives in schools, like the mackerel, and the kind that lives by itself, like the whale.

When first the savage drew a rude picture of a fish on his hut it was a whale, and not a mackerel.

We do not find the mackerel's picture excepting at the fish dealers and on the menu, and then only because the mackerel is good to eat.

Among trees the one that attains great proportions and beautiful symmetry is yonder giant oak or elm that grows in the open. It needs room to breathe and grow. It grows better if it is segregated from the crowded forest. The giant tree is not the one that grows in the dense forest.

There are two kinds of men, the kind that lives in the herd and the kind that has strong individuality that needs room to grow. The herd man exists in infinitely greater numbers than the individual man.

We cannot imagine Lincoln, Bismarck, Webster, Clay, Edison or Burbank living in the herd, or spending their time in the boulevard cafes.

The man who lives in a herd, who is ever present where the lights are bright, where gaiety abounds, where excitement reigns, where feasting is present, soon gets himself into the habit of cultivating this excitement. He is never happy when alone.

The brain never sleeps and something must occupy it. The herd man fills his brain with frivolous things, he seeks constant excitement. He is like the plant always in the sun, he burns himself out.

The great man with the individuality is great because he has always spent plenty of tune by himself, sizing up things in solitude. Sizing up things makes the brain grow and makes it stronger.

The universities of this country tend in a great measure to produce the herd man. The students dress alike. All have the same mannerisms, all have the same tilt to their hats, and all the same turned up trousers. They feed at certain restaurants and crowd in flocks. Very few college men learn the benefits of sizing up things in solitude until in after years.

On the other hand the student in the school of practical experience does not copy his fellow students. That is why in this great practical experience school we find Lincolns, Edisons, Jim Hills and Carnegies. Those men have to wrestle with the problems for themselves. They had to size up things in solitude instead of reading the sizing up from text books, as is done in the regular university.

Every man before retiring at night, or even during the day, should take a few minutes to himself and carefully analyze the doings of the day.

He should weigh the positive and negative acts, the good and the bad, the wise and the foolish, the right and the wrong impulses, the gain and loss in achievement. He should strike a balance, and if he sees that the bad, deterrent and backward things in the lead he should resolve to get a move on himself.

The man who goes along without this sizing up things in solitude is like the merchant who keeps no record, who pays his bills from the cash drawer and takes what is left for profit. He will still be running a little shop in twenty years, while his competitor who sized things up each day will be in the wholesale business or will have retired with a competency.

Try this sizing up things for two weeks, and the benefits you will receive will be so manifest it will need no further suggestion to make you keep up the practice.

Competition

The saying is "competition is the life of trade," and this saying is true, or it would not have endured so long.

If it were not for competition we should be living in the woods in a state of savagery.

Ages ago all men and women led the simple life. Their chief vocation was idleness. When the weather was hot the man sat in the shade; as the sunshine crept to him he moved into the shade again. In winter he reversed the process.

When our savage ancestor felt a pain in his stomach, his simple instinct showed him that if he put things in his mouth and swallowed them the pain in the stomach would leave.

This low browed man's whole object in life was to keep from having those hunger pains, and the only energy he expended was in hustling for food and in protecting his food from the other savages.

One day a man observed that the beasts lived on each other, so he conceived the idea that it would be good for him to live on other animals. That it would be easier than digging roots and gathering herbs, so this man caught and ate slow-moving animals. He used a club to do the killing.

Along about here competition began, for another man learned to throw a club and kill his game. Then another competitor discovered that a round stone was a more effective weapon than a club.

These hairy forbears of ours lived in caves until competition led up to the building of huts.

One day a savage discovered that while the skins of animals were hard to eat, they nevertheless made a good body covering. Another discovered that if the skins were tied about him it left his arms free to act. This man was the first tailor. He punched holes in the skin and tied the rude garment together with strips of skin. This first tailor was quite an important man among his fellows on account of his great discovery.

Some of these wild men were fleet of foot and had well developed cunning. They became expert hunters. On the other hand some of the less active, by the law of compensation, became more expert tailors, so trade was formed. The hunter killed enough for himself and the tailor, while the tailor made clothes for both of them.

In these days the woodsman lived on animals and the plainsman on vegetables mostly. So the woodsman traded skin clothing with the plainsman for grains and herbs, and this marked the birth of commerce.

Then dugouts and canoes were built, and thus our ancestors crossed lakes and seas and developed maritime commerce.

From away back in those dark ages up to the present time competition has stimulated mankind and spurred him on towards better conditions. The whole human race has benefited by each improvement which competition has brought about.

We have in mind a certain mail order house that up to 1894 had things its own way. Then it sold two to three million dollars worth of merchandise annually. A competitor came into the field, stirred things up, and now the old mail order house is doing eight to ten times as much business per annum as they did before they had the competition.

In the matter of competition we must early learn not to worry over competition, but to derive as much good from it as possible.

If a competitor does something better than you do, do not kick or protest, but jump into the band wagon and do the thing as well or better than he does it.

Price cutting is the simplest and most common phase of competition, but a better way to get advantage over your competitor is to improve your business by cutting off wastes and leaks, and reducing fixed and fancy charges so you can give your customers more quality and more quantity for the money.

In proportion as you increase the value you give for a dollar, just so you will find it easier to get the dollar.

Do not regard competition as hurtful to your business, but rather look upon it as a pace-maker for you.

If you had ten experts working for you studying how to improve your business you would certainly get benefit from it, but probably not enough benefit to offset the great cost of hiring these ten experts.

On the other hand, if you have ten competitors who are sitting up nights studying how to improve their businesses, you can get the benefit of their experience without it costing you anything.

The world is big and there is room for all, but old compensation says the prizes are given to the fittest.

If you are a laggard, if you are on the defensive instead of on the aggressive, get busy, wake up, do it now.

Advertising

Good advertising is good publicity. Advertising is the thing that makes your trade increase.

Everything you do in connection with your business and every act of yours outside of your business is an advertisement.

Reputation is an advertisement, so is honesty, politeness, correspondence, methods, catalogues, circulars and salesmen. Neatness is an advertisement, and so is promptness, thoroughness. And then there is another kind of advertising which is your statement in the newspaper. This is the printed kind of advertising, and this kind of advertising is the most common, in fact, when we suggest that you should advertise, it immediately comes to your mind that advertising is space in the newspaper.

Keep in mind, however, when we speak of advertising we refer to everything in connection with your business that makes an impression upon the public or the prospective buyer.

Some of the old timers refrain from printed advertising in newspapers, saying that the best advertisement is merit. Merit is a good advertisement, but it is mighty slow in its action.

If the inventor of the typewriter planned and built the machine in his barn without letting anyone know about it, if he kept absolutely quiet about his doings, relying on the fact that the typewriter had merit, it would never be known to the public unless he told about it. If the inventor of the typewriter waited for merit alone as the vehicle for acquainting the world with the merits of the typewriter, the world would never know of it, unless, perhaps, a fire inspector or an health officer accidently stumbled across the machine while inspecting the premises.

If the inventor waited for intrinsic merit to sell his goods, he would find that months and years would elapse before he could develop his business into profitable proportions.

If you have a good thing you must tell about it. Telling makes selling. Telling is advertising.

Professional men hold up their hands in horror when you suggest advertising to them. They tell you they don't believe in advertising, that it is not ethical, that it is not dignified. Doctors and lawyers are most notable in this respect. One of the first things of their code of ethics is "Thou shalt not advertise." They mean paid newspaper advertising. The man who originated this idea evidently did not have the money to pay for any, and it was a case of sour grapes.

Let us look into this matter of ethics and see whether the doctor and the lawyer really believe what they say about this matter of advertising.

It is a rare spectacle to find a lawyer who will not gladly give an interview to a newspaper reporter during some important trial.

The doctor gladly avails himself of the opportunity to read a paper before a medical society, and he sees to it that this paper is published in a medical journal later on.

Professional men belong to clubs, take part in public affairs, speak before people, work on committees, and actively take part in anything that will bring them in the limelight of publicity. They do this advertising themselves, yet they say they do not believe in advertising.

Uncle Sam builds war ships, equips his soldiers splendidly, conducts his business affairs with high grade talent, all this that the United States may be well advertised among our sister nations.

Advertising is absolutely essential to successful business. Not printed advertising alone but all kinds of advertising. The quality, the price, your aggressiveness, everything in your business is an advertisement, either a good advertisement or a bad one. It behooves you to see the advertising you do, whatever kind it may be, is of the good kind.

If you expect to remain in business a long time your advertisements must be good. Keep in mind that methods are advertisements.

One bad move, which is a bad advertisement for you, calls for two or more good moves or good advertisements.

Have everything, every detail of your business carry a good advertisement, that is, have it help your business.

Have every employe pulling on the same center tugs and have them all face forward, and your vehicle will move forward.

Buying

The buyer derives much information and much shrewdness by carefully watching the seller's methods.

Some buyers seem to think that bull-dozing tactics, cute lies and irritable manners make the seller humble, weak-kneed and non-combative. This is a great mistake.

The best buyer is first a gentleman. He keeps his word, he is patient and he knows his business thoroughly.

The buyer gains much by being open and above board with the seller. Let the seller know that your success consists in getting as much value as you can for the money, and that your continuous trade will result only through fair treatment.

Let the seller understand that the better he treats you in the matter of price and quality the better you will be able to treat your customers, and the longer you will be able to deal with the seller.

The moment a buyer shows bull-dozing methods, the seller is antagonized, and his object then is to soak the buyer.

The buyer who keeps his temper and goes at the matter philosophically is the one who wins out.

The buyer should explain to the seller that the seller can get the best of him once and may be twice, but not more than that.

The main thing for the buyer to possess is a most thorough knowledge of the goods he buys. Learn who makes the goods and where they are made, and get at the factory cost.

Then learn whose factories have the best reputation, and whose are the best fitted and established to make the goods you buy.

Remember you can afford to investigate. When you find a factory over-sold you will find that factory more independent. When you find a factory short of orders you will find them eager for your trade, and the chances are you can do much better with this factory than with the one that is behind on its orders.

Don't get excited, don't hurry. Speak gently. Know your ground. Cultivate a reputation for fairness rather than smoothness. Laxity and indifference in buying means that you are allowing wastes and leaks to creep in your business, and that you are placing a handicap on your traveling salesman, for goods well bought are half sold.

Expenses

If you get confidential with Mr. Bradstreet or Mr. Dun so that they will give you access to the inside history of the commercial concerns which have failed in business, you will quickly discover that in the majority of cases the cause of the failure was "too much expense."

It has become quite a common saying in speaking of failures that "the expenses ate up the profits."

Our friends Mr. Dun and Mr. Bradstreet tell us that there is about one concern in fifty which succeeds in business. If you will look at the successes you will find out that the proprietors were good buyers as well as good sellers but that the particular point that made them successful was their ability to make careful analysis in the matter of expenses.

The business man should have his expenses divided into as many classifications as possible. His payroll should be separated into various departments, office, salesmen, workmen, accounting, and so on; through all the items of expense the division should be made as finely as possible.

The proprietor should have a statement each week on his desk showing how every cent was expended. These items should be summarized monthly, and constant reference made to the items of expense in comparison with items of expense for the previous month, as well as items of expense for the same month of the previous year.

One of the pit-falls in nearly every business is "general expense" or "sundry expense." This department is a catchall for a lot of items, and it hides a lot of leaks and wastes in business.

You can't divide your expense items too minutely. The finer the divisions, the easier you can detect a waste of money.

The business man who has a statement of both receipts and expenses is in the position of the first engineer of an ocean steamer; he does not seem to be doing much and does not worry unless something goes wrong, then he shows his training and ability to mend breaks and repair weak places.

If the business man analyzes his sources of income into several divisions the same as he does his items of expense, he will find it an easy matter to correct errors that creep in the business. He does not have to worry about those items of expense which show minus, nor about those items of receipts which show plus.

With a finely divided sheet of both expenses and receipts you can quickly determine where the profit is coming from and where the leaks appear.

If an expense item shows plus, you can run down that item and see reasons for it and endeavor to bring down that expense. If a receipt item shows minus, you can run down that item and endeavor to increase the receipts.

The writer has a little printed card on his check book and it reads "Drive the axe into expenses." It is a constant reminder to stop the wastes.

The only real success that comes to the business man is the profits at the end of the year, that is, the amount of money he makes net.

It is easier to increase profits by cutting the expenses in many cases than it is to increase profits by increasing sales. And here let us remark that on this subject, as well as all the other subjects we are writing about in this series of articles, we have in mind the matter of common sense, temperate action. Extremes carry things too far. You must not cut the expenses beyond the point where it seriously interferes with the sales.

If you are interested in this matter of expense, and you certainly should be, take up your items of expense for last month or last year, go over the cost of help, the cost of raw material and the cost of manufacturing; go over each branch of your expenses, analyze the items carefully, look into every point thoroughly, and we will guarantee that at the end of your analysis you will see where you can save a respectable sum in the operation of your business. In going into this matter of expense, do not take all the items at once, but take each item up separately and go through it thoroughly.

Do not assume that you are paying too much for everything, but use good sense and good judgment and see that you get your money's worth. Take the item of wages. Look over the individuals in your employ, and you will see a place, for instance, where two persons can do the work three are now doing. Remember, it is generally true that where two persons are engaged in handling a certain department and they are overworked, the tendency is to give them additional help. When this is done you will find thenceforth all three are busy. In other words, each of the two persons who were formerly overworked ease up and do less work the moment the third person is given as assistant. You have noticed that where you put three employes to do the work formerly done by two, it is almost impossible—if you take the employe's word—to get two employes to do the work after three have been doing it.

The work should push the employe. The employer should get full capacity of his employes.

Look over your pay roll and make up your mind that here and there you are going to employes and ask them to help you save money, and at the same time you will let them earn more money for themselves. You will find that this plan works admirably.

For instance, if you have three employes getting $10.00 a week each; go to the two who do the most work and say to them: "If you can do the work of this department with one less employe I will give you each $3.00 a week more." In this way you will pay two employes $13.00 a week instead of three employes $10.00 a week each. This will save you $4.00 on that particular part of your payroll. If you save proportionately all through your payroll it will make a decided profit in itself.

Saving can also be made in the payroll by taking one of the heads of the department into your confidence and letting out the work to him by contract, offering to give him one-half, or one-third or one-quarter of the amount he can save in his department.

It is surprising to see how different his argument will be when his pocket is affected. For instance, in the past he explained to you that his department is behind in its work because he has not enough help.

He has been asking for more help right along, but never asked that some of the help be laid off.

If, on the other hand, you say to him you will give him one-third of what he can save in the matter of wages in his department, you will instantly notice that his whole argument and attitude change. He discovers that he has ability to pick out employes who do the most work, and lets out the four-flushers and idlers.

Remember, that as a rule the best paid employes are the cheapest. You can well afford to pay the heads of your departments more wages if they can save you more money.

A manufacturer should divide the number of completed articles done per day or per week by the amount of wages paid, and find out what the wage item is in each department per article.

Suppose that under your present system it costs you eighty cents in wages per article in Department A, sixty cents per article in Department B, etc. Explain to the foreman of Department A that it is now costing you eighty cents per article for wages in his department, and to the foreman of Department B that wages are costing you sixty cents per article in his department. Tell these employes you will give them one-third or one-half of whatever they can save in their departments. You will find Department A will cost you from seventy to seventy-five cents per article thereafter, and Department B from fifty to fifty-five cents per article, and in the meantime the foreman of the department is making more money for you, and likewise making more money for himself, than under the old system.

This matter of expense is most important, and should have the most serious attention of the proprietor.

Advice

One of the things most frequently asked for and yet one seldom made use of, is advice. Ninety-nine times out of a hundred the man who comes to you for advice as a matter of fact really wants to have his own opinion confirmed.

Do not go around with a pocket full of advice offering it to everyone. If you advise a man to change his habits or manner of life he will resent your proffered aid. The best way to give advice is to take another fellow for example and hit your friend through the illustration of the other fellow. Let him discover the point himself rather than let it appear that you are telling him the thing.

The matter of advice is a very hard thing to properly understand. You advise another to do a certain thing, forgetting in the meanwhile, that if you were in his position your view-point would be his and not your own. You play your strong qualities against his weak ones.

It is easy enough for you to advise a drunkard not to drink, but difficult for you to understand his view point on the subject if you are not a drinking man yourself.

Giving advice usually comes about because we see a weakness in others. The opposite of this weakness is a feature in our own make-up.

The business man who is constantly asking advice is advertising the fact of his uncertainty of his own actions. Your great problems must be decided by yourself.

The one thing that separates the sheep from the goats, and success from failure, is the ability to analyze, study and weigh problems for yourself, and to make decisions for yourself.

The law of compensation comes in here again, for in proportion as you have self-reliance and good judgment your success will be measured.

You may rely upon it that if you go about seeking advice, you will get two kinds of advice—First: the advice that concurs with your own preference or decision; and, second, the kind that is in opposition to your views. You accept the first kind because it tickles your vanity, and you throw aside the second, saying the advice is prejudiced.

Don't ask advice. Size up and weigh the problem yourself and use your own best judgment.

Reading

The business man who goes along day by day without taking on any responsibilities or without tackling more difficult problems, finds he does not progress.

The man who gets into a rut and reads light, frothy literature all the time—the kind that is pleasing to the imagination, the kind that leaves no permanent impression—does not progress mentally.

Reading should be like eating, we should have the dessert as well as the substantials. It would be a great mistake to eat dessert alone, and it is certainly a mistake to read light, frothy reading matter alone.

One of the prime requisites to a successful career is concentration of thought. Few things will dissipate thought as much as over-reading of newspapers.

The newspaper starts in with the first page, and by the time you have finished the last column oh the last page you may have read a hundred articles, each one of these articles touching on a different line of thought. The daily newspaper contains climaxes of all kinds. Each article is a distinct change of thought. The daily newspaper gives us statistics, sorrow, laughter, crime, passion, death, lies, humor, and so on all through the gamut of the scale of human experience.

The man who craves the newspaper soon finds his line of thought frequently interrupted, side-stepped, drawn, cut off and dispersed.

Abundant evidences are at hand where the book reader acquired the daily newspaper habit and reads the daily to such an extent that it is impossible for him to read books thereafter. He has broken his continuity of thought, and when this happens book reading is impossible.

Everyone should read two or three or more books at a time. One should be an interesting book, whether history, story or comedy, so long as it is well written and along lines that will hold one's interest. One should read one book after another of this sort as a dessert for his dinner, as it were, but along with it he should eat substantial food in the nature of substantial reading.

Do not read yourself to sleep at night over a light novel. Read your novel for an hour or so; then take up your old philosopher or scientist and read a page, or as much as necessary to find some thought clearly expressed so that it will be burned into your mind. That thought will remain and will be of service to you in years to come.

Read daily newspapers scantily. Read items concerning the business you are engaged in. Read the doings of Congress and the important events of the day. Go over the head-lines, if need be, and eliminate all those shocking stories of crime and sordid influence. Do not let yourself get into the habit of reading the details of horrible crimes and bad impulses and criminal acts. Skip over all the details of hangings and murders. They are weeds in the mind that choke up the beautiful flowers of thought.

Remember, everything you read depresses or elevates, and in proportion as you accustom yourself to read substantial matter so in proportion you will progress in this world, and have a flood of thoughts at your command when requirements come upon you calling for clean-cut expressions.

You will write better letters, you will converse better, you will enjoy social intercourse better if you read helpful reading matter from books and read newspapers very sparingly.

Argument

Not once in a thousand times will one man convince another in an argument, and the benefits you get if you do convince the other fellow will not compensate you for the waste of energy expended on the other nine hundred and ninety-nine times when your efforts failed.

You convince a man against his will and he is of the same opinion still.

There is a mighty lot of difference between argument and reason. You may accomplish more by dividing your case into one or two good reasons and telling your adversary that you will not argue the case, but you will let him look at these reasons, and when he takes it up logically you will have no fear of his conclusion, for truth must triumph.

While argument itself is a footless proposition, it is infinitely more so if your argument is with those of less mental calibre than your own, for by the law of compensation, in proportion as a man is ignorant, he makes up in perversity and lack of analytical ability.

Do not stoop to contend with those who have no standing, mentally, morally or physically. It is a waste of time.

If it is your purpose to change a man's opinion, do not try to do it by argument. Study the ground carefully. State your points with preciseness, make careful analysis of every phase of the situation, take up the matter point by point. Start with your adversary by getting on ground on which you both will agree. Take up the points on which there can be little chance for differences of opinion. You will find the other man will get in the habit of agreeing with your propositions and that his antagonism weakens. State facts that are right and truthful, and are so plain that the truth will be self-evident.

After you have made several propositions on which the other man agrees with you wholly, then make a proposition that is ninety per cent. his way and ten per cent. your way. Gradually increase that ten per cent. until you swing him around so that he sees the truth. He then imagines that he has made the deduction himself.

Remember, you can swing the biggest ship around by a steady, slow, gentle pull. On the other hand a sudden strain on the hawser would produce no effect whatever on the ship.

The man who wishes to convert another to his way of thinking must be a diplomat if he is successful. Do not get excited, keep cool and collected, be sure of your ground, be positive in your assertions, make the whole matter clear, and use good judgment, sound reason and clear logic.

Speculation

You are playing against odds when you speculate.

The only man who has a sure thing on the Board of Trade or Stock Exchange or the race track is the man with the "Wienerwurst" privilege.

The successful business man some day wakes up to the fact that his bills are paid, and that he has surplus money. This surplus money should be used for investment purposes and not for speculation. Of course, it is hard to draw the line where investment leaves off and speculation begins.

When you speculate on margins you are like the fellow holding on a bear's tail as it runs around a tree—if you lose your hold the bear will get you.

The man who makes an investment, buying stocks or real estate and paying cash for them does not have to worry about the market. Prices may be up or down, but the man who has paid for what he has bought will sleep well.

You can't beat the speculation game. The only ones who make a success, and their success is ephemeral, are those who make speculation their whole occupation. The professional speculator is merely a high grade gambler, and he always winds up a loser.

Go to the Stock Exchange or the Board of Trade and you will see at either place a half a dozen old fellows hanging around. They are all men who have seen better days. A little inquiry and diplomacy on your part will bring forth the fact that these men were once prominent figures on 'Change.

When you have more money than you need in your business buy good farm lands out west, or good timber lands. No man ever bought good farm land or good timber land at the prevailing market price and lost money eventually. Of course, at different seasons of the year the price of land may go down a little temporarily, but the moment a good crop comes in, the price goes up again.

With good clear farm land you can always go to the nearest bank and borrow from sixty to seventy-five per cent. of its value.

Real estate is the true basis of wealth, and if you want to play a sure game, buy land that produces things.

When you buy vacant property in a large city, it is mere speculation. The land does not bring in any remuneration, and you are simply betting that the prices will increase.

Every large city has abundant instances of vacant property that is not worth as much now as it was ten or twenty years ago. Real estate booms come in cycles. Prices go up and men get the fever and buy vacant property. The boom explodes, property goes down and you can't get your money back. The chances are you have bought the property on two or three years' time, and it certainly is paying for a white elephant when you are paying for land that is worth less than what it cost you. You cannot get out, however, because the original payment has already been made, and your only hope is to save something on your investment.

Notwithstanding the fact that certain business sections and certain residence sections in any city steadily increase in price, yet the average real estate in the city increases by very slow percentage. The same amount of money, put out in mortgages, with the interest added and compounded, will develop wealth greater than the average vacant property investment, for where one lot soars up to a high price there are a hundred that don't increase at all, and the picking out of the lot that is going to increase in value is as hard as picking out the horse that is going to win the race. It is because the vacant city property has only speculative value that the business man should not touch it.

Buy farm property that you can rent. It will bring you interest on your money right along, and the tendency of farm land is and always has been steadily forward.

Mr. Yerkes, of Chicago, was a speculator who made millions in the street-car system. He was thoroughly familiar with Hydraulics, and he soaked the stocks as full of water as possible and then unloaded on the investors who speculated in street-car stocks. These speculators are now holding the bag. When Mr. Yerkes closed out his holdings in Chicago he granted an interview, and one truth he uttered in that interview has ever been remembered by the writer. It is so valuable an expression coming from such a successful speculator that we are going to give it to you. It is as follows: "I have never known a business man to successfully speculate in grains or stocks for two years."

The business man who is watching the ticker or calling up the Stock Exchange every day, who takes little flyers, is skating on mighty thin ice.

When you buy farms you are exchanging your money for the most certain thing in the world, for the basis of all wealth is land, and money simply represents the things which come out of the land. The things that grow on the land are exchanged for gold, and the gold is exchanged for things that come out of the land. The Government exchanges the gold for pieces of paper called money, which in reality means that you can exchange these pieces of paper for gold, and you can exchange the gold for the things that come out of and grow upon the land.

The stock broker may not like this chapter because the more speculation the more he benefits. He gets a rake-off every time a man buys and every time a man sells. He plays a sure thing. He is like the man with the Wienerwurst privilege.

Don't Speculate. Invest.

Elimination

One of the greatest brain savers is elimination. Every man should try to operate along lines of the least resistance, eliminate the deterrent influences and all things that fret him.

Do not look for trouble. Do not concern yourself too much over disagreeable things over which you have no control.

Do not build up an intricate system in your business. Have simplicity your ideal. Eliminate all useless moves. If you have disturbing influences in your institution, such as an employe who is continually causing friction, eliminate that employe. The man who causes friction is pulling back on the forward impulses of your business, and he is holding back one or more men who are trying to help you forward.

Get rid of useless things that take your time or cause you worry.

Remember that as you grow successful people will come to you under various excuses to get your aid financially or morally. They want you to go into new companies. The officers of the Club to which you belong will ask you to be a director. You will be invited to dinners, asked to speak, asked to do a thousand and one things, and in proportion as you accede to these demands you will find the demands increasing until finally you have little time to attend to your own affairs or to attend to your family.

Have as your center idea—elimination. Everything that takes your time from your business or your family is an extra tax on your strength.

Eliminate every habit that holds you back, every practice that unfits you for progress, every person who depresses you, every move that is not necessary, every footless idea that crowds your brain.

The Specialist

When this nation of ours was born nearly every one was a generalist.

The merchant sold a general line of merchandise. The doctor was also a farmer and a horse trader. In those days there were very few specialists.

As time passed some of the wiser individuals turned specialist and succeeded.

The doctor who is a generalist cannot excel in any one branch of medicine, or compete with the specialist who devotes all his time and study and practice towards one point and towards the treatment of a specific ailment. The merchant who sells everything cannot compete with the man who makes it his business to sell one class of goods. This is an age of specialists, and what we considered a specialist twenty-five years ago is only a generalist from the present standpoint. The specialist of twenty-five years ago has been divided again and again. The best doctor today is one who doctors the eye alone, the stomach alone, or the nerves alone. He can do more for you and knows more of your case in five minutes' observation than the generalist would in three months.

With the keen competition of these days it is necessary for the individual to be a specialist in business.

Pleasure and recreation are the only things in which an individual should be a generalist.

Were it not for specialists we should know little about the sun, little of electricity, little of steam, little of railroads, little of advertising, little of anything else. It is because individuals have made a speciality of one thing, because they have concentrated their energies and their brain power on one thing that the world has progressed.

Recreation is for relaxation, and the business man should see to it that he gets the full benefit of recreation. If he carries specialism into recreation, recreation is spoiled, for the moment a man is a specialist in recreation he strives to excel, and this striving to excel is hard work, and that is the same thing he is doing in business.

The business man who plays billiards and no other game doubtless will play a better game than the generalist who indulges in all sorts of games and recreations, but the man who makes a specialty of billiards finds his powers centered on this game of billiards. He puts his thought on it and wishes to excel, he wishes to make a record, and billiards then become business.

This striving to excel in a game brings forth the same gambling instinct manifested in business. It is his "I will." The business man who plays a good game of billiards some day meets his superior, and the superior is the individual who does nothing but play billiards.

If a man tries to be a specialist in billiards and a specialist in business, even though both callings commence with "B," he will find that a division of effort is a division of results, and he will not be a success in either business or billiards. In proportion as he excels in billiards he will be lacking in business, and vice versa.

We remember the story of a young friend of Herbert Spencer who joined the great philosopher in a game of billiards. The young man played a most excellent game. When they had finished Spencer remarked: "Young man, your education has been greatly neglected, you play billiards too well."

Be a specialist in business and a generalist in pleasure. Play billiards, swim, ride, play golf and indulge in all athletic sports and so long as you get uniform pleasure and recreation from these things you are doing right, you are helping your mind and developing your body and letting your brain rest, so that it may be keen and a greater help in your specialty, which is business.

The world needs specialists, and it needs specialists in recreation as well as business, but the man who tries to be a specialist in business as well as a specialist in recreation will fail in both, or, at least, his success will be only moderate.

It is necessary for life's scheme that we have individuals who have steady incomes so that they do not require to enter the strenuous business life. It is necessary to have such individuals, so that they may devote themselves to being specialists in recreation, otherwise the sports would die out.

If you go in for sport do not expect you can compete with anybody who goes in for sport exclusively. You can't win in two callings or occupations.

The String

There is a string to every proposition, and it behooves you to look out for the string before acceding to the requests that are made of you.

When a stranger comes and offers to do things for you, to let you in on the ground floor, or assures you that he is working for your interest, you may be sure there is a string to his proposition, and the string is that, as a matter of fact, it is himself instead of you he is looking out for.

Don't bite at the chance that is offered you to get something for nothing. The biggest kind of a string is always in such a proposition.

Remember this, that people are selfish. Each man looks out for his own interest, and even if he is protecting your interest, it is because his own interest will be better conserved by looking out for yours.

Don't decide on important matters too quickly. Don't get tied up in big contracts with strangers until you have found every strand of the string.

Don't be too suspicious but hunt for the string. It pays to be very conservative on all matters in which others are interested.

Sometimes the string in the proposition is legitimate and the other fellow may be more interested than you are, but it certainly behooves you to see what this string is and to understand exactly where the end of the string is tied.

Don't draw up in your shell and look upon every man with a proposition as trying to take advantage of you, but put down this as a truth—There is a string to every proposition, and you must find that string before you close the deal.

Horse Sense

Just how the expression "horse sense" came into use is not known, but the meaning of the combination means good reason, old fashioned logic, simple analysis and actual truth, and the basing of your actions upon simple things rather than complex things.

The man who uses horse sense in his transactions gets along further and faster than the man who uses selfishness and smartness.

To be possessed of horse sense is a most valuable asset. It is something you can use every day of your life.

Horse sense is really one of the things that makes up the law of compensation. The law of compensation itself is the quintessence of horse sense.

Luck is the gambling chance, and horse sense is the investment and security chance.

The man with horse sense may not go as far in a day as the man with luck, but he will progress more days and go further eventually than the lucky man.

Horse sense is one of the most valuable things in the business world, and it is one of the rarest things. It is so valuable because it is so rare.

In the business world today the men who are doing great things are the men who have horse sense. We call these men wonderful and look upon their accomplishments as the result of some mysterious, wonder-working power that they possess. Wonder workers are only flashes in the pan.

Do not hire your employes on account of your preference for a certain color hair or certain colored eyes. Do not hire your employes on account of their physical appearance, or on account of their ability to dress in the height of fashion. Get down to their net worth. Find out how much horse sense they have. Hire employes, as far as possible, who are blessed with old fashioned horse sense.

The Manager

The good manager is one who commands respect, not through his authority but because those under him appreciate that he has more ability and experience than they have.

The selection of a good manager is very important, for the success of one's business depends upon its management. The proprietor cannot do all the things himself, and he must rely upon his lieutenants.

Give a certain class of work to ten girls. Put them in a room by themselves with no one in authority. Come back next day and you will find that there is one girl who is laying out the work for the others. There is something in this girl that makes her a natural manager, and there is a certain instinct amongst the rest of the girls that makes them acknowledge this one girl as their superior, and the one to go to for advice. This natural leadership is the quality the manager should possess.

Above all, the manager, like the boss, must know how to do things he hires others to do, and the things we have said concerning the boss is likewise true of the manager, for the manager is the next step below the boss. The successful boss would not have obtained his present position if he had not been a good manager previously.

Let the manager read thoroughly our chapter on the boss if he has ambition to be boss some day.

The mistake frequently made by the manager is to take credit himself for the work done by those under him, for such a manager may be sure that sooner or later his position in this respect will be found out, and to his surprise he will find that the employe who has been doing the things for which he has taken credit will take the manager's place. Employes are quick to detect this spirit in the manager. They see that their own efforts are not known to the boss, and it makes them indifferent, because they see no appreciation for what they are doing. On the other hand, if the manager says a good word to the boss concerning an employe who has shown marked ability, it redounds to the manager's credit that he is liberal enough to give credit where it properly belongs.

Truth will out as sure as the sun will shine, and the manager cannot conceal his subordinates' abilities and pass them off as his own for any length of time.

The good manager will say a kind word to the boss about the employe, if he is the right sort. It makes an employe feel confidence in the manager when he knows that the manager is appreciative and ready to tell his superior of good things in the employe's favor. The manager who is bad tempered, suspicious and tries to take credit that does not belong to him is only holding his position temporarily, and some day he will be let out of the institution for which he is working, and will find himself forced to the extremity of getting a place somewhere else back in the ranks from which he had temporarily risen.

Selling

Time was when the best salesman was the one who could tell the biggest lies, drink the most whiskey and show his customers the liveliest time.

Today the best salesman is distinguished by the following attributes: Truth, trustworthiness, together with a fine knowledge of the goods he is selling.

The man who sells goods must be prepared to hear from nearly every man that his price is too high. If the buyers would always tell the truth, then the salesman who sold the most goods would simply be the one who actually sold at the lowest price.

Price does not mean anything. Price is high or low only when quality is taken into consideration.

The man who sells merchandise, or advertising, for instance, must be thoroughly acquainted himself with the thing he sells. He must be reliable, he must give good measure, he must keep his word.

We hear a good deal about the live-wire, rapid-fire salesman, who goes out on his initial trip and comes back with a bagful of orders. It must be remembered that ever and always there is the law of compensation to take into consideration. The salesman who bags a lot of orders on the first trip does not get so many the second time. He has colored his picture too highly on the first trip. He has made too many side promises, too many mis-statements, and the customer finds out he cannot be believed, and this smooth article of a salesman is not as welcome in the buyer's office the second trip.

On the other hand and in strict accordance with the law of compensation, the salesman who tells the truth, who moves quickly, who does what he agrees to and knows what he is talking about, who talks convincingly and attends strictly to business will eventually succeed.

The great house of Marshall Field & Co. of Chicago have operated along the line of fairness, good treatment and willingness to right a wrong and correct a mistake quickly. Marshall Field had horse sense when he inaugurated his business.

Wonder workers who start out with a burst of speed and smash records in the matter of selling will still be salesmen at fifty years of age, for you can't go fast far.

Those wonder workers change frequently. They flit from house to house. They work because they need the money to have a good time with, and as soon as they get the money they proceed to have a good time until their little pile runs out, and then they get another job. Business men know this wonder worker well. Go into any wholesale house and you will find them. They are living in the past and relating their conquests. They never speak of the present but always of the past. They have done things they can't do again. The good salesman is doing things now better than he has done in the past.

The permanently successful salesman does not cut much of a figure in the matter of dress. He is not as handsome as the wonder worker. In fact, he may be physically uncouth, but he has a heart under his rough exterior. The customers he mingles with have confidence in him. They know he will do what he promises, and finally this man is the one who builds up a good trade and at fifty years of age he has a place of his own, sends salesmen on the road, and his house does a good business because his policy permeates the institution, and the customers have confidence in the house because he is at the head of it, and they are familiar with his methods and practice.

Some buyers seem to think that it is necessary for them to give the impression to the seller that they are buying at lower prices than the seller quotes. The wonder worker tries to make each customer believe that he is buying at the lowest price. The common sense salesman does not resort to such tactics.

The average buyer does not concern himself so much about being able to buy cheaper as he does to feel sure that his competitor does not get better treatment than he does.

In the matter of selling there is no one thing that ultimately proves so successful as the one price plan. By that we mean the same price to all who purchase the same quantity or the same amount in a given time.

The more elastic and variable your prices, the more ingenuity required to keep these cut prices from getting into the hands of your customers. This matter of cutting prices causes no end of worry. In proportion as you indulge in cutting prices, so in proportion you will receive an increased number of cut price offers.

Let it be known that your prices are subject to reduction at the hands of a smooth buyer, and the news will travel fast.

Let it be known that you don't cut prices, and that news will gain currency in the trade, and you will not have cut prices offered you.

There is something in the matter of selling beyond dollars and cents, and that is dollars and sense.

Remember this, when you sell goods you are also selling reputation. If your goods are bad your reputation will be bad too. You can't have a good reputation and sell bad goods and make a permanent success.

Remember, every sale you make is an advertisement.

Remember, you can take advantage of the buyer once or twice, but if you want to hold his trade you must be fair with him.

Smooth tactics that bring in present money react and lose trade for you later on.

Vacations

Every man owes it to himself and to his family to take a vacation each year.

Vacate means to get out or away from, and if you take your so called vacation by a trip to another city and spend your time in the whirl of industry, you are not helping yourself, you are not taking a vacation. Neither are you resting your mind and body if you go to a swell summer resort where white duck trousers in the day and full dress in the evening is the rule.

The real vacation you get is when you take yourself away from the business marts of trade, and go to a place where you can get your feet on good old mother earth. Go where fences are unknown, where there are no "keep off the grass" signs, climb the hills, walk through the forests, fill your lungs with good ozone, say to yourself "all these beautiful things are mine."

Nature has arranged it so that the poorest man in the world can get the most priceless things as easily as the multi-millionaire. The four most precious things in the world are good air, good food, good water and good health. Money cannot buy any one of these things. The man with millions cannot get any better air, or more nourishing food, or purer water, or better health than can the poor man.

The man who goes to the big woods for his vacation, who lives out of doors, who gets near to nature, is putting by a reserve in his constitution and brain that he will draw upon for the remainder of the year. Such vacations will clear the cobwebs from your brain. It will give you ability to do greater things, and make you see the beautiful side of life.

A man should not depend wholly on his two or three weeks in the woods, however. He should take a little vacation every day. He should arrange to get some benefit for his brain and body in each twenty-four hours. He should take a few moments each day and devote it to mental and physical relaxation. And, above all, he can get a good vacation every twenty-four hours if he sleeps properly.

Our good friend Grizzly Pete, of Frozen Dog, understands the real vacation when he says.

Mighty pleasin' sport, you bet, sittin' on a rock;
Beats a store or office an' workin' by a clock.
Clears away the cobwebs from your weary brain;
Gives you inspiration; makes you a man again.

There ain't no medicine I know for the appetite
Like a summer mornin', waitin' fer a bite.
Lazy summer days are here—ain't you kind o' wishin'
That you had your old clothes on, an' was settin here a-fishin'?

Health

There is no misfortune, no real hard luck except sickness and poor health.

If you find your health is becoming impaired, change your methods and vocation. Change before it is too late. A stitch in time saves nine times nine in matters of health.

Get plenty of exercise, good air, good water, sleep with your windows open in winter as well as summer, walk over two miles every day. Avoid worry. Do good deeds. Help others. Eliminate evil thoughts and deterrent influences.

If your health is impaired, forsake dollars if necessary and make health your first concern.

Dollars are worth having, but sense is infinitely better to be possessed of.

If your health will not permit you to get dollars and cents, then make it your object to get health and sense.

Rockefeller would give his millions if he could have the health of nearly any of the thousand of employes who work for him. A good stomach is rather to be chosen than great riches.

Patience

Supposin' fish don't bite at first,
What are you goin' to do?
Throw down your pole, chuck out your bait,
An' say your fishin's through?
You bet you ain't; you're goin' to fish,
An' fish, an' fish, an' wait
Until you've ketched a basketful
Or used up all your bait.

Suppose success don't come at first,
What are you goin' to do?
Throw up the sponge and kick yourself?
An' growl, an' fret, an' stew?
You bet you ain't; you're goin' to fish,
An' bait, an' bait agin,
Until success will bite your hook,
For grit is sure to win.

Patient effort and hard work each day, properly directed, will surely bring success.

Failure comes to those who grow weary in the struggle, and to those who overwork themselves and overtax their abilities.

Such persons hope that by large sacrifices of sleep and happiness, and by extra application and hard work, they will build for themselves fortune, that they may be happy at some future time. They make a great mistake in this respect.

Divide your energies so that each individual day is successful, no matter how much the success may be.

It is the men who are doing little things today who will be picked out to do great things tomorrow.

And while you are making a little success each day, be sure that your heart sings while your hands work.

Men who can do things are discovered. They need not push themselves to the front. Good men are scarce, and the great successful business men of today are the ones who know how to do the work that they are hiring employes to do. Talent in this direction will surely attract the attention of your superiors.

Learn to master the details of your business yourself. Use conscientious effort and painstaking effort. Make a round-up each night of what you have done during the day. See wherein you have been in error and wherein you could have improved the day's work and you will be better fitted for tomorrow's duties. After closing your day's business, devote a part of the evening to your family and friends, and a part of it to some good book.

It is not the clock that strikes the loudest that keeps the best time. The expensive chronometer works steadily along doing its work well and faithfully. It does not attract as much attention as the gilt clock with its sweet chimes, but men who know things are aware that the chronometer has the more real merit. Have the chronometer for your ideal and not the fancy clock, for true merit will certainly receive due reward.

We should all have some ideal which we hope to attain tomorrow, but let us remember that the way to reach the ideal tomorrow is to make today successful.

Patience is a virtue few of us are possessed of, but the story of every successful business has written on every page of its history patience and perseverance.

Do not get discouraged if your rate of progress each day is not as much as you hoped for, but, so long as you are going forward and are patient, you may be sure that you are gaining.

Hard Times

Hard times follow good times with unerring regularity and certainty; this is in perfect accordance with the rule of compensation.

In good times we should prepare ourselves and erect strong guards around our business, so that when hard times come we may find ourselves able to go through the troublous times.

If prosperity ran on unchecked, the ordinary, well-established business would soon be a thing of the past, for people would speculate instead of work.

When the manufacturer has his bills paid and finds a surplus in the bank, that surplus is likely to be turned into speculation. When everyone speculates values rise, and continue to rise until prices reach fictitious altitudes, and then comes about the cashing in. It so happens that the cashing in is a general movement, and when this happens hard times quickly follow.

The successful business man should keep his money where it is get-at-able, and when hard times come and the prices go away down to low water mark, then he should buy. Later on prosperity will return, as sure as the sun will rise, and the things bought during the hard times will greatly increase in value.

Hard times and prosperity rotate several times in a man's business career.

Hard times are necessary to the general scheme, for with continuous prosperity business would increase to such a momentum that there is no telling what the results would be.

In times of prosperity you must make preparations for the hard times that are sure to come. If your pumps are greater than your leaks, your craft won't sink when the storm of adversity and hard times breaks across your ship.

Sleep

No one can do his best work if his mind is wool gathering. If an employe is thinking about the races, he is cheating his boss, for he cannot give him his best service. If the employe is in the habit of being up late nights, he cannot concentrate his mind nor bring out the best there is in him. Nothing is so good for the hard worker, nothing will stand him in such good stead, as plenty of sleep.

Go to bed early. Get lots of sleep every night and you will be ready and strong for the fray of the morrow. If you get plenty of sleep you are far ahead of your fellow employe who does not get enough sleep.

Sleep smooths out the wrinkles, builds up a storage battery in you and gives you confidence in yourself. You hold your head higher, your step is more elastic, your eyes are clearer, your mind works better, and your stomach does its full duty if you have taken plenty of time for sleep, for sleep is the plan of nature to restore the mind and the body.

Lack of sleep means wilful waste of your energies and a dulling of your abilities.

Business men pay for ability, keenness, alertness and capacity, and in proportion as you limit these qualifications by lack of sleep, so in proportion will your salary be kept down.

Grumbling

Grumbling kills friends. The business man who is ever grumbling and growling about things makes a blue atmosphere about him. People somehow or other seem to prefer a rosy atmosphere to a blue.

There is no good in grumbling. It gains nothing. Grumbling is an evidence that you have not sized things up correctly. That you are laboring under a delusion; that you are looking at the world through blue glasses, that you are not making proper estimates of other people.

Grumbling is an advertisement to the world that you are not well balanced. Grumbling won't help things a bit. The more you indulge in the habit the more firmly it becomes fixed upon you, and later you will find it almost impossible to shake it off. The grumbler grows to be a pessimist; he says disagreeable things; he makes his friends feel ill at ease. The grumbler gradually loses his acquaintances and even his close friends.

If you are starting on the grumbling path, pull yourself together and cut the habit quick and short. Grumbling and indigestion go hand in hand. If you have indigestion, square yourself against it, make up your mind you will not indulge yourself and vent your ill feelings in grumbling.

If you can start out each day with a resolve not to grumble you will find the proposition not difficult. The first two or three hours of the day is the time when your resistance is called into play. There is no better antidote or cure for the poisonous grumbling disposition than the following, which has been for many years a pet sermonette of the writer: Be pleasant in the morning until ten o'clock, the rest of the day will take care of itself.

Associates

"Birds of a feather flock together." "A man is known by the company he keeps." "Like begets like." "We are creatures of environment."

All these truthful sayings have been preserved as proverbs simply because they are simon pure truths.

The matter of associates is most important for the business man or employe to consider. The young man who spends his time in gambling, drinking or dissipation cannot do his best work. He can no more hide these practices than the clouds can obscure the sun permanently, for evil, as well as truth, is sure to come out.

One of the best attributes a man can possess is character. Character gives him credit at the bank, it gives him a standing among men. If the employe ever expects to be a boss he must have character, and he must associate with men of ideas who will be helpful to him.

A man will never improve his game of billiards if he always associates and plays with an inferior. He may satisfy himself for the time being that he is a big toad in a little puddle, but if he plays with a poorer player than he is he is bound to retrograde.

The only way we can advance is to surround ourselves and associate with uplifting influences and healthful individuals. Our eyes should be turned forward and not backward.

It will make several seconds difference in the speed of a horse whether he is running against a horse he can beat or running against a horse that can beat him. Race horse men have reduced this truth to actual practice. They have what is called a pace maker. When they want a horse to trot fast they mount a boy on a running horse just ahead of the trotter.

If a man associates with his inferiors, the association will surely keep him from progressing.

If you want to make money, if you want to progress in the business world, go where money is being made and mix with people who are making money.

No man is naturally bad. No man gives himself over to criminal acts or hurtful habits solely upon his own instincts. These actions and habits come about through associations.

Go to the criminal court any day and you will see evidences of the man who is pulled down on account of his associates.

Mix with your superiors in matters of business and morals and you will unconsciously absorb qualities and ideas that will push you to the front.

Hitch your wagon to a star. Aim high. Pick out ideals in business, and eliminate from your path all deterrent influences. There is no hold-back like harmful associations. You will be judged by the company you keep.

Old dog Tray was really a good dog, but he suffered because of his propensity to associate with bad dogs.

Fixed Charges

Fixed charges are sums you have to pay out regularly, week after week, or year after year. When you buy materials and supplies, when you lease property or hire employes, or pay interest on borrowed money all such things are fixed charges, and it calls for the best there is in a man to keep these fixed charges down as low as possible. When you buy a single item, such as a desk or a chair or a waste basket, do not lose a lot of valuable time trying to save too much on those articles.

When you go to New York once a year, do not stay at a second class hotel for the several days you are in New York, when by the expenditure of fifty cents a day more you could stop at a good hotel.

It is false economy to spend five dollars' worth of time to save fifty cents.

When you are buying single articles that are not fixed charges you have a little more leeway in the matter of price than when you are buying things that come under the head of fixed charges.

In the matter of fixed charges the penny you save on the unit assumes vast proportions in the many multiples.

Some men will deny themselves a respectable desk because they can buy a cheaper one for ten dollars less, and this same person will lose a thousand dollars through laxity in buying things that come under the head of fixed charges.

If you buy one lead pencil never mind whether the price is five or ten cents, but if you buy great gross lots every few weeks you can afford to be very circumspect and painstaking in the matter of price.

If you are buying a shirt, fifty cents one way or the other does not make much difference, but if you are in the furnishing goods business and buying thousands of shirts at a time, twenty-five cents a dozen means quite a lot.

The matter of stationery and printing comes under the head of fixed charges. If you are buying letter paper for your personal use and you require but three or four hundred sheets in the course of a year, don't bother very much about the price per quire. The stationery you use in your business, which you buy in large quantities, you should be careful of. Plain, respectable, good quality letter paper is the kind used by successful concerns. The fancy-colored, freakish paper is nearly always used by the four-flusher in business. He is trying to put on a good front. He uses hand made paper and hand made envelopes. All the get-rich-quick people use fancy, high-priced stationery.

The successful house uses a good quality of linen or bond paper, and a medium grade, regular stock size envelope. Envelopes are thrown away; letters are saved. That is why an envelope does not require to be as good quality as the letter. It is the letter and what you put on the letter that cuts the ice.

Fixed charges usually hide a lot of little leaks. Stop them. Many little leaks make a big aggregate in the course of a year, and there is no place where these leaks start as easily as in the matter of fixed charges.

Cigarets

We cannot call to mind a single instance where the habitual cigaret smoker got to the top of the ladder and held his position. We see heads of large establishments smoke cigarets, but the habit was acquired after the position was attained.

The cigaret smoker suffers from lapses of memory, his nerves are shattered, his judgment is not good, he forgets things and is irritable. He cannot hope to compete with the clear-brained individual who does not smoke cigarets.

It is not the cigaret itself that does the harm, it is the smoke inhaled into the delicate lung tissue. This smoke covers the lungs with yellow nicotine, carbon and poisonous gases.

Some men smoke pipes because they wish to escape the criticism to which the cigaret smoker is subject. The pipe smoker who inhales does himself more injury than the cigaret smoker who inhales, because the pipe smoker takes in more smoke.

Go to the medical college dissecting room and see the lungs of a man who inhaled smoke, and you will quit the habit if you have been guilty.

Don't burn your lungs with cigaret smoke, or pipe smoke either.

The fight to get to the front is hard enough anyway, and if you want to win, do not poison your blood with tobacco smoke.

Return Good For Evil

One of the first laws was "an eye for an eye and a tooth for a tooth," but as time went on and man developed mentally his animal instincts were subordinated and the law was changed, and the new law was this: "return good for evil."

Nearly every man who has an injury done him tries to repay the injury. He must either repay it with good or with evil. If he repays it with evil he does not get satisfaction. If he repays it with good he gets happiness. It is certain that payment of evil with good can satisfy a man who is looking for revenge, while it has always been a question whether there is any satisfaction in paying evil with evil.

If a man does you a mean turn he is expecting you will repay him in like manner. He guards himself against this. He is ready for your revenge, but if you repay him with good you attack him in a weak spot and make him feel like thirty cents, and this is all the revenge you can ask for.

It is all right to get square with a man who does you a wrong, and the best way to get square is by doing him a good turn.

You should keep mental ledger accounts with all of your friends and all your enemies. When a person does you an injury, debit him until you have a chance to credit his account with some good turn; when you credit his account be sure you overpay what you are owing him, so you will have a balance coming to your credit.

We have been taught to return good for evil, but we have heard the saying so many times that few of us pay any attention to it.

It's worth while testing, this rule of returning good for evil. The next time someone harms you, repay him by doing him a kindness, and see if you don't feel happier, and at the same time get all the satisfaction you are looking for. It matters not whether the person to whom you have done a kindness appreciates it; you have been benefited and received happiness by your own act, for virtue is its own reward.

The man who returns good for evil, has the satisfaction of the man who has on clean underwear, the world may not know it but he does, and that is all that is necessary.

Learn to Play

Nature has given us many positives and negatives. It has given us the ability to work hard, and it has given us the ability to play hard. Work while you work and play while you play. The man who is successful is the man who works hard during business hours, and then goes home and leaves his office behind him and takes up play.

A man should devote a part of each day to recreation, to outdoor exercise, to frivolity and to frollicking with his children at home. If he does not care to play, worry will take the place of play.

Worry and hard work together will kill a man. Work and play will make him live.

No two things can occupy the same space at the same time. These brains of ours are always busy, and we should be careful what we give the brain to act upon.

If we work hard all day, the tendency is that in the evening the brain revolves the things that have been going through it during the day. A review of these thoughts produces worry, especially if our occupation has been a strenuous one and if things have not been to our liking. When we devote ourselves to play, then worry and brain rack will be absent all the time we are playing. Play was made to rest the brain. Your sleep will be better if you have indulged in recreation, and your mind will be clearer the next morning.

Good Fellowship

Call a man a fellow and he will resent it, call him a good fellow and he feels complimented.

The good fellow is ever found where pleasures abound. He shines at the dinner. His knowledge of mixed drinks is a revelation.

The good fellow spends his time where the glasses clink, where the horses run, and where the revelers congregate. His earnings go for dinners, bottles and shows, and while these occupy his mind he imagines he is having a good time, that his actions evidence "good fellowship."

Go to the clubs and you will see the "good fellow." He is spoken of by all the other "good fellows" as a "good fellow." And they are all good fellows together.

Some day the good fellow is taken sick and dies. He has not a cent to his name, and the other good fellows take up a collection to bury him. The only persons at the funeral are the other good fellows, and the only requiem he receives is "Well, he was a good fellow."

The good fellow at fifty is working for the good business man. The good fellow is like the butterfly, and sips life's pleasures, and shows off his fancy colors, living for today only.

The successful man is like the ant, he works and puts something away each day, where he can get at it in the future.

When winter comes with its chilling blasts, the butterfly has nothing in reserve and it starves to death, while the ant keeps himself alive on the product of his own labor.

Some day the good fellow finds himself in need. He goes to other good fellows, but they can't help him because they are in the same boat themselves. Then our good fellow grows pessimistic, and finds out too late that it does not pay to be a good fellow.

Good fellows don't get good jobs very often. When they do get them they don't hold them very long.

It is a mighty poor recommendation to be referred to as a good fellow. People seem to think that the words "good fellow" cover a multitude of sins, and when a man has done wrong, or makes a mistake, or uses bad judgment, the other good fellows try to excuse his faults by saying—"Well, he is a good fellow, anyhow."

The good fellow bursts upon us with his halo about him. As time passes the halo dims and the good fellow peters out.

The good fellow who is so popular at the Club today is found tomorrow trying to eke out an existence selling books and life insurance to other good fellows.

There is nothing in good fellowship that can be negotiated at the bank. The credit man of the wholesale house does not give credit on good fellowship.

Hard Work

It is a mistaken idea that hard work kills men. Hard work never killed a man. It is the improper care of oneself when he is not working that does the damage.

The more a man does with his brain the less his hands will have to do. The better a man's reasoning and common sense are, the more successful he will be. It requires hard work these days to keep up in the race.

You cannot make a success unless you work hard. Hard work will be much easier if you keep worry out of it.

Hard work brings success, but to do hard work, the machinery must be in good order. You must keep your constitution up, you must have plenty of sleep and you must learn to eat and breathe properly.

No story of success has ever been truly written that did not depict hard work in every line.

Success comes by inches, not by leaps or bounds. Success is the pushing forward each day by hard work.

Burn the candle at one end only and you replace each day what you have burned, by rest, sleep and recreation. By burning the candle at one end only and replacing it fully each day, your candle will not burn out.

Kindness

"A little word in kindness spoken,
A motion or a tear,
Has often healed the heart that's broken
And made a friend sincere."

There's nothing in business that pays so well as kindness. A man may spend his money, and in proportion as he spends it he reduces his principal. With kindness the matter is different, for in proportion as you spend kindness your principal increases.

Lincoln said "You can catch more flies with a drop of honey than with a gallon of vinegar."

Kindness is beautiful. It brings round you many persons who are ready to say kind words to you. This subtle, potent influence of having lots of friends to help you by their actions and showing their hearts is a great blessing. It is surprising that people know so little of the value of kindness.

The word "gentleman" is really a compound word, meaning gentle-man, and these words together in their simplicity are the true definition of the word gentleman.

Kindness means gentleness. No man is a gentleman who is not kind.

People are glad to recognize goodness and kindness in an individual. No one can act the part if he is not sincere. We must cultivate kindness, if there is little of it in our makeup. We must take an inventory of our qualities, and if the weeds of mean impulses are crowding out the delicate flowers of kindness, we should pull out those weeds and give the flowers a chance to grow.

Lincoln was a kind man, kindness was his chief delight, and his examples of kindness have been of untold benefit to millions of people. You remember he said, "When they lay me away let it be said of me that as I traveled along life's road I have always endeavored to pull up a thistle and plant a rose in its stead."

Life at best is short, and the only things we really get out of life are happiness, health and love. Money cannot buy these things.

The trouble with many business men is that they imagine good examples and kindness have no place in business. They think the time to be kind is after they have attained success financially. They think the time to show kindness is outside of business hours.

The real way to be happy is to do the thing now, live each day for itself. Get kindness in each day.

The man who is grave, austere, the man who tries to skin the other fellow, who devotes all his energies to money-making alone, finds as the years go by and he has attained his goal, but that he does not know how to enjoy himself.

There are three periods in a man's life—the future, the now and the past. When we attain old age our life is largely made up of reminiscences, or looking back over the past. If our past life has been one of struggle, worry and getting the best of the other fellow, then there is little happiness in looking back over such a life.

The true philosopher does the thing now, he lives each day. He puts kindness into his action, and when he grows old, he can look back through a life that was pleasant as he lived it, and pleasanter now in living it over again.

One of the Greek philosophers expresses the following beautiful thought: "If there is any good deed I can do, or kindness I can show, let me do it now. Let me not defer or neglect it, for I shall not pass this way again."

The trouble is that some of us keep our kindnesses, or rather the expression of it, until it is too late.

We should remember—"Do not keep the alabaster box of your love and tenderness sealed up until your friends are dead. Fill their lives with sweetness, speak approvingly cheerful words while their ears can hear them; the kind things you mean to say when they are gone say before they go. The flowers you mean to send for their coffins send to brighten and sweeten their homes before they leave them. If my friends have alabaster boxes laid away full of fragrant perfumes of sympathy and affection which they intend to lay over my dead body, I would rather they would bring them out in my weary and troubled hours, and open them, that I may be refreshed and cheered by them while I need them. I would rather have a plain coffin without a flower and a funeral without an eulogy, than a life without the sweetness of love and sympathy. Let us learn to anoint our friends beforehand for their burial. Post-mortem kindness does not cheer the troubled spirit. Flowers on the coffin cast no fragrance backward over life's weary way."

The Salesman

Selling goods or soliciting requires careful study. The salesman who makes the greatest success in the long run is the man who has practiced truth and established himself in the confidence of his customers.

The whirlwind makes a good showing on the start, but, by the law of compensation, what a man gains in speed he loses in power.

Some customers are slow to open up and extend their confidence to a salesman. Others make up their minds quickly and express their preferences.

A great deal of preliminary work can be avoided if the salesman is tactful on the start. First impressions are lasting, and a salesman should study carefully his first appearance. He should be neatly but not flashily dressed. He should be a gentleman above all things. The gentleman dresses so that later we can not accurately describe the clothes he wore. It is the flashily dressed salesman we can describe later on, for his clothes are so out of the ordinary that they are remarkable in this respect. The flashily dressed salesman is remembered by his clothes rather than by his personality.

The solicitor should never smoke in the presence of the customer on first acquaintance. The matter of smoking in a customer's presence has prejudiced many a man against a salesman who has this practice. Business men have prejudices, and to some smoking is highly obnoxious. Under no circumstances smoke in a customer's presence unless the customer is smoking, or until at least you are well acquainted with him, and have received his permission to smoke.

Times without number the writer has left his half-finished cigar in the hall-way before entering the customer's presence.

Story telling is like a two-edged sword; sometimes it helps and sometimes it is a distinct disadvantage to tell stories. You must know when to tell stories, and, above all, do not tell stories to your customer that he could not repeat in his home.

Above all things, the salesman must know his man. If the customer gives evidence that he is fond of a story, then remember a good story and tell it to him. No salesman ever made a distinct hit by telling vulgar stories. While a customer may laugh, he forms an opinion of you that is not complimentary, and, if you are always telling stories that you would not repeat where women were present, the customer forms a very low estimate of your character.

The facts are the world is full of good stories, and good stories help your case, while vulgar stories hurt it.

Drinking is another method used by many salesmen to gain favor with a customer, and what we have said about vulgar stories may be applied to the matter of drinking.

Years ago it was a general practice to take the customer out and get him half seas over before trying to sell him.

The customers who are most susceptible to influence through whiskey are the ones who are most likely later on to cause you trouble, either through failure in business or through their preference for some other individual who can outdo you in the matter of drinking.

You must get your customer by the heart and not by the stomach. You must make your customer believe in you.

In these days the business man likes to deal with a salesman who is business from the start. He only buys goods because he expects to make money on them, and the sooner the transaction is over, the sooner he can turn his attention to other matters.

The best advertising solicitors and best salesmen are those who get business on business grounds and through their knowledge of their business, rather than through their ability to tell stories, order dinners and drink liquor.

The good salesman studies the other side of the question. He acquaints himself with the method used by the customer in disposing of his goods. He does not talk his own side of the case all the time. He works with the customer, tries to give him good advice and shows an interest in the customer's business. Such a salesman gets close to the customer, and retains his patronage long after the good fellow has passed away.

Be wise, be patient, and above all things, acquaint yourself thoroughly with the goods you are selling. Know more about them than your customer does. Live up to your obligations. Keep your appointments. Study your customers' welfare. Help them when opportunity offers.

The life insurance solicitor who gets the most turn-downs is the one who writes the most policies, because the fact he gets so many turn-downs is owing to the fact that he has seen so many people.

Hard work, cheerfulness, honesty, patience, sobriety and knowledge of good goods will make a man a successful salesman.

Honesty

Under this caption we are expected to say "Honesty is the best policy." This expression is as old as the hills, and if it were not good it would not have obtained so long, for honesty certainly is the best policy.

Many a man in business practices absolute honesty and integrity, because honesty is the simplest and best method he knows of for doing business.

No man can succeed permanently, who is dishonest in his practices. The successful business man is the one who practices honesty in all actions and dealings during his business experience.

Honesty begets honesty. The man who is honest in his dealings with his fellowman has a subsidy which money cannot buy. He gets honest treatment at the hands of others.

The merchant who cuts a bolt of silk in the middle and puts different prices on each piece, may figure he is making money by his action, but retribution is sure to follow.

Honesty is a slow road to wealth, but, in accordance with the law of compensation, in proportion as the business built up on honesty is slow, so in proportion will it last longer.

Honesty is the best advertisement a man can have in his business.

Success

If after the employe strikes a balance each day, he finds that he is moving forward, then he is on the road to success. And so it is with the business man, only the proportions are greater.

One cent put at four per cent. interest per annum nineteen hundred years ago, with interest added to the principal every twenty-five years, would represent today more money than there is in the world. It would have taken twenty-five years before the original investment of one cent was doubled.

If a man had started that plan his grandchildren would have said the scheme was no good because it was too slow.

The boy goes to school regularly and shows little advance in his mentality if you measure from day to day, but the boy is gaining every day. He is going ahead slowly but certainly.

The gambler and the foolish man like success to come quickly and with great strides. It is because there are many foolish men and gamblers that the get-rich-quick fake thrives.

The man who gets rich suddenly usually indulges in such sports as lighting cigars with ten dollar bills, and his wind-up is in the pauper's grave.

No man knows the true value of money unless he has worked for it. The man who has earned his dollars through the penny route knows the value of the penny, and he gets mighty good value when he spends a dollar.

The man who walks steadily in one direction does not appear to be making much progress. The ship on the ocean seems to be standing still. When night comes the man who has been walking steadily has disappeared, and the ship that seemed to be standing still has vanished beyond the horizon.

The law of compensation says, The more haste the less speed, and so in the matter of success, we must not feel discouraged because the speed at which we are traveling forward does not seem noticeable when compared with the rapid pace of some of our friends.

Be not impatient. Learn to wait. Be a good stayer. Do not let the success of the get-rich-quick creature deter you from your resolve to move forward slowly. You will get there in the long run.

And when your hair is silvered and cares rest easily upon your shoulders, the long road you have traveled will be a source of infinite satisfaction to you. Your retrospection will be pleasant, and the very things that were hard in your youth, are sources of satisfaction to you in your old age.

Do not use the yard measure in counting your progress, but use the inch rule that has fine fractions on it.

Thinking

"I did not think" is an excuse offered by many. Thinking is the thing in business.

The trunk railroad, the trans-Atlantic cable, the steam engine, the electric light, the wireless telegraph, the very republic in which we are living, came about through thinking.

Every man should take from five to fifty minutes each day to divorce his mind from the strenuous activity surrounding him, and devote that time to thought, and good will come out of it.

The brain is like a muscle, it must be exercised or it becomes flabby.

Cultivate concentration of thought; study your sphere of usefulness; cut out the weeds that grow in your brain; get out of the mental rut you are in; stop drifting; keep your brain healthily active.

Men are paid either for what they think or for what their muscles do. Man's muscles have a limit; he can move just so much matter by physical force. But his capacity from a mental standpoint is unlimited.

The world offers golden prizes to the man who thinks. Therefore we should cultivate our brains and make them expand. The brain is like a plant. If you nourish and cultivate it and care for it, it will grow too.

Excitement, striving for pleasures, indulging in reading light, frothy literature, excessive daily newspaper reading are all weeds and thought killers.

Don't act on impulses. The get-rich-quick man or the fake mine promoter says, "Buy today, the price goes up tomorrow." These fakirs don't want you to think. Thinking is an enemy to their persuasive arguments. If you think, and think rightly, the fakir does not get you.

When you get a nasty letter don't answer it right away. Think it over. Think carefully. If your thoughts of revenge are so strong that you cannot calm yourself down, then write a letter and express yourself in the fullest degree. Leave the letter on your desk. Do not look at it for three hours. Then when you look at it you will instantly determine to tear it up, because in the meantime you have been thinking.

Thoughts expressed on paper have a different sound than if they are uttered verbally, therefore you should think carefully when you write.

Cultivate poise, calmness, and practice careful thought before you speak or write.

In proportion as you master difficult problems through thought, your brain will be ready for greater conquests.

Here are some things to think about during these times when business is so good.

These prosperous times are dangerous times. In times of prosperity we build up false idols, and raise our hopes and ambitions beyond the safety point.

Prosperity makes most of us careless. We don't give our business the careful consideration we should. We run to extremes during prosperous times.

We should make the most of prosperity while it is here. We should enjoy it to the fullest, but we should remember that for every high tide there is a low ebb.

Prosperity should enable us to put away a reserve for the hard times.

We should be careful that prosperity does not turn our heads or cause us to lose our vigilance.

Home Life

After all we say and do, the real pleasure of this world comes from the home. The gilded palaces we see in our travels abroad are beautiful to look upon presently, but later on they serve their purpose to make a contrast with the sweet simplicity of home.

When you go home, cut business out, and let play and sociability and love occupy your time.

A married man should be in partnership with his wife. The man being fitted with sturdier physique, with strong ability to combat, should take up the heavy burden of business, for those are the things he can do the best. The wife should take up the home part of the duties of the firm, and when evening falls each member of the firm should try to lessen or take away the cares to which the other has been subject during the day.

The best place in the world is the home, and in proportion as home life is unsatisfactory or uncongenial, so in proportion are the Clubs filled with dissatisfied and unhappy men. If you want to hear pessimistic talks on home life, talk with those derelicts who spend most of their time at the Clubs.

Learn to make much of little things. Learn that smiles and good humor in the home bring happiness, and iron out the frowns and check the mean impulses arising within us. Be pleasant every morning until ten o'clock, and the rest of the day will take care of itself. Start out in the morning right and happiness will be home at night.

There is nothing in your old age that will be such a comfort to you as retrospection, or looking back over a long life of happiness in the home. The happy little incidents which today seem trivial will be remembered in the future, and a thousand and one occurrences which are happening in the home are being put away in the store-house of memory, later to be called upon and enjoyed again.

In the evening of life when you and your silver-haired partner sit before the fire place, when you have retired from active participation in your respective branches of the business, which is bread winning on the part of the man and bread making on the part of the woman, then you will have a happiness and satisfaction which all the gold in the world could not buy. The pleasures of the old who have had happy homes during their lives are the greatest pleasures in the world.

The sunset of your life will not be beautiful unless your home life was pleasant during your day of work.

Optimism

The man who is an optimist may be laboring under a delusion, but certain it is that he is happy while under the delusion.

Every man should have ideals. He should see the beauty and good in things. He may not accomplish his ideals, but the anticipation and working out of them is a mighty pleasant vocation.

The pessimist is always unhappy, and when no definite thing is before him to worry about, the very fact that there is nothing to worry about makes him unhappy.

The pessimist says "Business is not half as good as it would be if it was twice as good as it is." The optimist says "Business is twice as good as it would be if it was only half as good as it is."

Grizzly Pete, of Frozen Dog, Idaho, is an optimist, and Webb Grubb, of the same town, is a pessimist. A short time ago they had a big rain storm in Frozen Dog. Webb Grubb kicked about the rain. Grizzly Pete, all wreathed in smiles, said "Rain is a mighty good thing to lay the dust." A few days later the sun came out oppressively warm. Webb Grubb kicked about the warm weather. Grizzly Pete, again all smiles, said "Hot weather and sunshine are mighty good things to dry the mud."

The pessimist goes about with a dark lantern peering into out-of-the-way places, ever looking for meanness and things to find fault about.

The optimist goes about in the bright sunlight looking for the beautiful things, and sees more things by the aid of the great sunshine than the pessimist can find with his little dark lantern.

The optimist rises in the morning with gladness in his heart, sunshine in his face and smiles upon his lips. The mere privilege of living and enjoying nature is a priceless satisfaction to him. He gets good out of life every moment he lives. He is a man to be envied, if envy is ever allowable.

The pessimist warps his mind and his physique, and his influence on others is decidedly bad.

The optimist raises the average of the world by his presence, the pessimist lowers the average.

The optimist is in the majority, however, and the world is growing better.

Learn to see beauty in the small things. Study nature. Watch the processes of plant life and animal life. Surround yourself with helpful influences; books, music, friends.

There is no investment a man can make that yields such unbounded returns as optimism.

Optimism cannot be bought with money. It is as free as the air we breathe. That is why poor people generally are optimists.

Memory

The man whose memory allows him to play four games of chess blindfolded is good for nothing else.

Book-keepers who can name every folio page and every customer's balance are good for little else.

There is nothing in mental gymnastics from the dollar standpoint.

The good lawyer or the good business man does not rely on his memory, but rather his ability to find out things and get at results.

If you remember only the customers who are slow pay or shaky, it will be a lot easier than to remember the names of all the customers who pay promptly.

If your wife wants you to get something down town tomorrow, write her request on a little piece of paper, roll it up in a ball, put it in your pocket with your loose change. Forget the incident, let the paper do the memory act.

Next day when you reach in your pocket for change you will find the little ball with the reminder on it.

If there is something you want to attend to at home, drop yourself a postal card.

Carry a little pad of paper in your pocket. Write down the little things you are to do. Don't store your mind with these temporary matters. Let the tab remember for you.

Let your mind be like a sieve, and have the meshes coarse enough to keep in the big things and let the little things go through.

Have your business figures written down, your comparative sales, increases or losses. Study the written figures. Have system. Do things methodically. Don't trust to your memory. If the thing you see or hear is worth keeping, write it down on the little tab.

The orator who commits his speech to memory is in a sorry plight if he forgets a sentence.

If you are to speak at a dinner, lay out your plan, divide your topic into several parts. Jot down the catch lines, and just before you speak look over the ticket. Charge your brain with the points or ideas and build the words around them.

Don't remember things with verbatim correctness. Remember the skeleton thought, the idea.

When you quote a price or figure, jot it down. Confirm the verbal statement by a written memorandum.

Memory is a bad servant sometimes. You remember a thing one way and the other fellow remembers it another way. You are both honest, but one of you is wrong. If you had made a memorandum in duplicate or jotted down the figures, what trouble it would have saved you.

Where dollars are concerned it is good sense to trust to a written memo., and not to any mental memo.

No use to cram your brain with transient things, when lead pencils and paper are so cheap and so easily obtainable.

The employe who trusts to his memory hurts the business, and after he quits a lot of misunderstandings will come up.

Insist on your employes making memorandums of things and prices, for when the employe goes he takes his memory with him. If he has a memorandum you know the facts.

Worry

Nothing will prevent effective work like worry. If you are given to introspection and worry, and allow these things to go unchecked, they become habits with you, and while your sleep, in a measure, is an antidote for worry, yet the more worry you have the less soundly you will sleep, and consequently the less effective sleep will be in correcting the injury caused by worry.

Sunshine and darkness cannot be present at the same time, for in nature one of the first rules we find is that no two objects can occupy the same place at the same time. No matter how much one is given to the worry habit, he experiences reflex moments when he does not worry. Some of our pessimistic friends who are given to the worry habit say it is impossible for them not to worry. You are thinking of what you are reading, and if your mind is interested in it you are not worrying while you are reading these articles, and this shows that if you are interested in reading there is little chance for worry to get in; for your mind is occupied.

Men have tried all sorts of things to escape worry. Some of them frequent places where gaiety and mirth abound, so that they are for the time being banishing worry, but in proportion as these things keep one from worrying, the reaction is stronger when it does come, and the individual who tries to escape worry by going the pace and occupying his time with light things, suffers more keenly from worry when it does come. Some men turn to drink to kill worry. Many a man imagines while he is drunk and his brain is clogged with alcohol that he is the happiest man in the world, and some of them go to the extent of imagining their finances are in a flourishing condition. The alcohol fills the brain with fancy pictures, and for the time being the mind forgets to worry. When the alcohol wears away the brain takes up the worry again in an increased degree.

To kill worry by the active process is like trying to cure rheumatism by external application. The only thing you do is to stop the pain temporarily. The best way to cure rheumatism is to go at it through the blood. Eradicate the uric acid from the system, and then the rheumatism will disappear. The best way to cure worry is not by local applications, but by getting at the root of things. Eliminate as far as possible the things which cause worry. Remember that as long as you live there will come things across your path that are not to your liking. You should be philosophical, and make the best of things that are about you. Look at the bright side rather than the dark.

There are only two things in the world to worry about. First—the things we can control or change; second, the things over which we have no control. Now, it is manifestly useless to worry over the first kind; for we can correct the thing and there will be nothing to worry about.

It is manifestly useless to worry over the things we cannot control, for, as set down in the second proposition, we cannot change the things. It therefore behooves us to eliminate from our calculations the second kind of worry, for no amount of worry can possibly change that kind. We must therefore confine our attention to the first kind, the kind we can change, and when we have changed the thing there is no cause to worry.

Nothing helps a man's health so much as contrasts in climate or habits. When the doctor tells you it is necessary to go to California or Arizona, or some other distant point, he knows that fifty per cent. of the good you will get by the change is from the water, air, sunshine and surroundings, and the other fifty per cent. of the good you will get is because you have been taken away from the very things that have been causing you worry. If you can't get contrasts by trips to other distant points, you can get the contrasts right where you live. If your mind is occupied in the day with deep thinking and hard business problems, you should occupy your evening with something that will contrast with it. Take up some light literature, play with your children, or work at some hobby in which you are interested.

The trouble with those who worry most is that they have worked themselves up to such a frenzied state they can't read anything excepting startling newspaper articles and freakish, frothy books.

The man with rheumatism cannot cure himself in a day, neither can the man with the worry habit eradicate worry from his make-up in a day or so.

The man who worries should make up his mind he is going to read and get interested in the reading. Let him set apart ten minutes the first day, and agree that he will devote those ten minutes honestly, intently to the subject before him. The next day he can add a minute or two, and so on until he can read one or two hours at a time. Finally, the wrinkles will be ironed out and the horizon will be brightened.

As we are, so is the world to us. The most familiar objects change their aspect with every change of the soul. When you worry, everything is distorted, everything appears unnatural, the world looks dark, our friends seem far off. The jokes we hear fall flat. We indulge ourselves in pessimism.

When the whole matter is summed up philosophically, there is no bad luck in the world except sickness. All other so-called hard luck is simply temporary. If you lose your money, don't worry about it, make some more.

If you lose a friend, don't worry; show him his mistake. If you lose an opportunity, do not worry; be ready for the next one.

Life is short. The end of life is death. What's the use of worrying.

Worry is like drink. The more you give it the more it fastens on you.

Cultivate a cheerful disposition. Mix with people who are cheerful. Do not allow the garden of your mind to grow up with worry weeds.

Occupation kills worry. If your mind is filled with uplifting work or brain training it will have little time to worry.

Promises

A business man may be rated as worth a million, but if he breaks his promises regarding payments or fulfillments of contracts, he will find later on those who deal with him will insist upon cash transactions.

Keeping promises is the basis of credit. Let it be said of you that you always keep your promise; that you have never been known to break your word, and you will need little persuasion to get the credit man's O.K.

If you purchase for cash right along, some day you can ask for and will receive a small credit, if you promise to make your payments on a certain date. If you keep your promise you can repeat the operation. Later on you will be given larger credit, because you have been keeping your promises. You can increase your credit step by step to amazing proportions if your promises are always kept.

The business world places much confidence in promises. The note in the bank is a written evidence of the promise. The note says on the face of it "I promise to pay." The Government of the United States issues bank notes on the face of which is a promise.

When you make promises as regards dates, jot down the promise in your memorandum book. Whatever you do, keep that promise. The man who breaks his promise in little things will break them in greater ones.

When you make a promise to meet a man it is just the same as promising to pay a man money. In either instance you are in the man's debt, and the obligation is not cancelled until the debt is paid. In other words, until the promise is fulfilled.

Just so sure as the sun sets, the man who habitually breaks his promises will surely break his business.

Independence

It seems to be the rule rather than the exception that the moment a business man attains success he grows independent.

There is no such thing as independence within the full meaning of the word. Every creature in the world is dependent more or less.

The man who takes delight in his so-called independence and forces it to the front, soon receives knocks.

The constant tapping and knocking hurts anyone. Boosts beat knocks. The man who has a reputation for being independent never gets boosts.

Some business men forget the obligations they are under. They forget the help that was extended to them in time gone by. They furnish up a fine mahogany office, with an outer room, and outside of this another room with an information desk. They cultivate coldness and independence. They make it difficult for their friends to see them. They put a lot of red tape around their business, and by these acts they get out of touch with the pulse of the business. They look at things through colored glasses. Their judgment gets warped.

In proportion as a man cultivates independence and autocratic ideas, just so in proportion is he nearing the brink over which many have fallen to destruction. When an independent man has a fall, his enemies glory and loud are the shouts that arise from them, and if we listen closely we will hear the multitude say: "Serves him right."

There is nothing like democracy in business. By this it must not be understood that the head of the concern is to see every pedler, or every life insurance agent. But if the business man is accessible, and greets you with a glad hand, and in the pleasant manner turns you over to the proper department head, you go away from the office satisfied, and you give this man a boost instead of a knock.

The late P. D. Armour was a good example of the point we are making, he did not waste time in social visits during business hours, but anyone who had business with the Armour Institution could get an interview with Mr. Armour. It has often been remarked by business men that they would rather have a turn-down from Mr. Armour than an order from some of the other houses, for Mr. Armour always made one feel good.

No one can be independent. The larger one's business is the more the proprietor is dependent on those around him.

It takes many months to build a sky scraper, yet a wrecking company can tear a sky scraper to the ground in a few days, and so it is with a man's reputation. It takes years to get good credit in the commercial world, but if success spoils a man and makes him independent, he has created enemies, and there is no telling where these enemies will get in their work. It is like the worms eating through the bottom of a ship. Some day the craft goes down because of the silent attacks made in it, which were not visible from the surface.

Some day the independent man is surprised to have the bank call him in and insist that he take up his loans. He is astonished; he does not know why this sudden change has happened, but like as not some secret enemy in the bank, or some secret competitor who has a friend in the bank, has gotten in his work, and then this independent man finds out how really dependent he is.

The safer a man is from attacks, the safer his business is from the financial standpoint, and the more generous this man should be in his consideration for others.

No man can afford to be independent. Men who have built up their business slowly are not the ones whose heads are turned and who affect this independent air. The independent man is nearly always the newly rich or the suddenly successful business man, and the moment he sets himself up as independent he is made the target for an army of enemies who are waiting for a chance to injure him.

Short Letters

Most business men make much ado about nothing in the matter of correspondence. They use a wilderness of words to express themselves. They write at such length that the original meaning runs into so many by-lanes that the meaning is lost.

The man who writes long letters usually deals out high sounding phrases and customary paragraphs such as he has picked up through his perusal of others' letters.

The average business man seems to glory more in his ability to use euphonious sentences than to talk to the point.

Letters should be like telegrams, they should be short and to the point, so there will be no misunderstanding on the part of the recipient.

There is one business man that we have been in close touch with for over fifteen years. We have heard from him an average of once a week, and in all that time he has never written a letter of over twenty-five lines. Our records show there is no customer with whom we had so much business dealings and so little misunderstanding as this one.

Write short letters. Use small words. Don't be blunt, but be short.

Perspiration

No matter what one's aspirations may be, success will not come without perspiration. It is well this is so, otherwise success would not be appreciated. That which a man earns by perspiration he appreciates and knows how to enjoy.

If success were something that could be drawn by chance, like a prize, success would not be worth anything.

The measure of any valuable thing, or condition, or relationship is the amount of work, energy, trouble and sacrifice that has been expended to obtain it.

None is to be more pitied than the rich idle-born, who have every comfort around them. They do not know that perspiration must be added to aspiration before they get success.

Friends

How little the average business man understands this word "friends."

In everyday conversation we hear one man say to another "Mr. Blank is a friend of mine."

As a matter of fact the word acquaintance could be substituted in ninety-nine cases out of a hundred where the word friend is used.

Real friends are few and far between. A real friend is never determined until a test has been made, and this test is usually troublous times, adversity or the loss of a loved one.

When afflictions come to our families, or reverses come to our business, when the dark clouds hang over us, when stormy seas are about to swamp us, when we need help, then is the time we find who are our true friends. When such calls for friendship arrive it is surprising to see how we have been mistaken in individuals. Those upon whom we counted most shrug their shoulders, draw their skirts about them and give us good advice, while those whom we had never counted as friends come to the front and lend helping hands.

The word friend has been greatly abused. Around places of gaiety, where drinks and good fellowship abound, we frequently hear the word friend, but in the time of trouble those who pose as friends will not help us, and the few who would help us cannot because they have squandered their substance and have not the ability to help us. A friend in need is a friend indeed.

There is no relationship more sacred than friendship.

Friendship carries with it love. The true friend is not one made in a hurry. There is no friend like the old one with whom you went birdnesting in your youth, the friend that has plodded along life's road with you shoulder to shoulder.

When you have a friend who has proven himself such, never let up so long as you live in your evidences of gratitude for the kindness he has shown you. Repay him with interest for his good offices, and let your actions towards him ever be a source of happiness and pleasure to him.

Nothing is so much appreciated between friends as gratitude, and nothing will kill friendship like ingratitude.

Genuine friendship is such a rare jewel that when you have a positive demonstration of it, let it be your great concern that you will do nothing to mar this friendship, for broken friendship is a source of grief to both friends so long as they live.

Employes

The success of any business depends upon the hearty cooperation of the employes.

We have often heard that a corporation has no soul. A corporation probably has no soul but most of us forget that the officers of the corporation have souls and hearts, and in proportion as the individual at the head of a corporation or private enterprise treats his employes just so he will be repaid.

We are paid back what we pay out. If we are harsh and mean to others, ever suspicious, ever looking for evil motives, those who work for us will be suspicious of us and look for evil motives behind our every act.

The employer who shows consideration, cultivates respect and sets a good example will find it pays from a monetary standpoint, as well as in the satisfaction he has in knowing that he is doing the right thing.

Lincoln said "A house divided against itself must fall." If the employes of an institution spend their time in wrangling and quarreling, it means a divided house, and the house will certainly suffer.

Set a good example to your employes. Take them into your confidence. Recognize ability. Advance worthy ones, and you will find everyone from the office boy to the officer pulling on the rope in the same direction, and you will get full measure of ability from everyone who works for you.

It is impossible to suddenly get a perfect working force. A good organization comes through the process of evolution and elimination.

Whenever an employe does all he is hired to do and a little more, that employe is in a position to occupy a place of greater responsibility.

If an employe is a sluggard or a four-flusher, he may be sure these things will be found out and he cannot hope for advancement.

Employes should remember that the most successful institution is the one whose managers are developed from the rank and file. The best houses do not hire high class help from other concerns. The most successful men are those who started in at the bottom of the ladder, and by perseverance and pluck and aptitude they climbed the ladder until they reached the top.

Employes should remember that the most difficult problem the employer has to solve is that of good employes.

A small want ad. in the metropolitan daily will bring an army of cheap help. The market is full of cheap help, but good employes that are worth over $2,000 a year are very scarce. The high priced employes are generally the best money makers of the institution, for they are selling their brains rather than their hands. The hands are limited, the brains are not.

Employes, there are golden opportunities before you. Disregard the clock. Bend your energies toward doing your work well. The advancement will be sure to follow.

The trouble with many employes is that their minds are filled with outside matters of a frivolous nature.

In every large city there are thousands of dude employes, the kind who wear high collars, the kind who spend all their salary for clothes.

The dude employe stands in his own light. He wears a higher priced tie than the boss; he is immaculately neat; he looks like a fashion plate, but at the same time his tailor bill is not paid, he is owing money right and left. He spends his evenings in the cafes, and at odd moments during the day he dodges out to look over the racing form and smoke a cigaret. This dude employe sits up late at night. He spends his salary, and more too, in the gay life. He is tired next morning when he comes down.

The dude employe who wears a high collar is not the one that knuckles down to hard work. Perspiration and high collars do not go well together. The dude employe does not like perspiration, so he sees to it that he does not exert himself enough to perspire.

Employes should remember that very truthful axiom: "The employe who never does more than he is paid for is never paid for more than he does."

The employe should remember that the boss takes large chances in hiring help, for there is not one employe out of ten that is a good investment. The employes should remember that it is necessary for the boss to make a good margin of profit on each employe, else he could not maintain his business.

Every employe who studies how much he can do is a help to an employer. Every employe who sees how little he can do is a hold-back to the institution.

Employes should remember that prosperity goes in cycles, that it is but three generations from shirt sleeve to shirt sleeve.

Over ninety per cent. of the bosses today started in and worked their way up from the ground. The young man who inherits a partnership in his father's business really has a handicap on him, and is not as likely to succeed as an employe who starts in at the bottom of the ladder.

Employes should remember that responsibilities only come to those whose shoulders are broad enough to bear them, and when additional responsibility comes to an employe that employe should look upon the responsibility as a distinct advantage to him, for it gives him an opportunity to show the stuff he is made of.

Laxity

When young men start in business their thoughts are all prospective. They look forward to the time when they will attain success. They work hard. They put enthusiasm and long hours into their business. As years pass they attain success and cash in this world's goods. They buy beautiful homes and surround themselves with luxury. They indulge in high living. They have country places. They take things easy. They sit back in their chairs and imagine their business will go on forever because they are so well established.

The hard worker is entitled to slacken up a little as success comes to him, but the moment his energies commence to wane, he should see to it that he gets the right sort of young material in the institution to keep up the enthusiasm and hard work which he himself has had.

In the very nature of things it is impossible for a man to keep up his youthful pace in his mature age, for, as we have frequently observed, you can't go fast far.

One of the principal elements in Marshall Field's success was that he got enthusiastic, hard workers around him. The moment he saw signs of laxity in any of these individuals, he let them out and got new material.

Laxity means loss of power, and with loss of power the machine does not do as good work.

Laxity in business is a waste.

Enthusiasm

In these days of keen competition and wonderful activity it is necessary for the business man to have enthusiasm. If he lacks in this, his business will be at a stand-still, while his enthusiastic competitor goes forward.

Enthusiasm should not be carried to an extreme any more than any other good thing should be carried to an extreme, but at that it is better to be over-enthusiastic than not enthusiastic enough. No one can be truly enthusiastic who does not believe in his business. Enthusiasm is a form of advertising. It shows the people you deal with that there is something going on and that you believe in your own medicine.

Catching Up

Nearly every one in this business world seems to be engaged in the occupation of "catching up." Nearly everyone is a little behind in the matter of finances.

As soon as one gets across the stream and is on dry land and has his bills all paid, then he takes on new responsibilities and goes deeper in debt.

It is a very hard game, this catching up. The game of existence is very easy to play when you are caught up.

We have tramped through the forests of the great West, and we have invariably found that the pace-makers or leaders are the least tired at night, while the followers or those who are behind trying to catch up, are the ones who are most fatigued.

Some people are habitually behind "with their hauling," as the Missourians say. No matter how their salaries may increase they are proportionately behind with their hauling all the time. When an employe gets $50.00 a month he is owing $75.00, he is working hard at the catching-up game all the time. He figures that if he only got $75.00 a month, he could apply the $25.00 extra and could catch up in three months. The theory is all right but the practice is not, for when this individual gets $75.00 a month, instead of applying that $25.00 extra to catching up, he finds that he wants better neckties and better underwear, and makes greater expenditures all along the line, so instead of wiping out that $75.00 debt he had when earning $50.00 a month, he finds himself $150.00 in debt on his $75.00 salary.

This catching up has a bad influence. It worries the individual; he does not do his best work.

When you have all your bills paid and a surplus of $500 in the bank, your head is higher, your chest is broader, your backbone stiffer, and you have a confidence that helps you take on greater responsibilities.

To be in debt is to be under obligations to your friends, and it kills off those strong qualities which you naturally possess but which warp when you are catching up. The man who is catching up cringes instead of standing erect, he is suppliant instead of dominant. He is disturbed by little things, and in the meantime the catching up process is tearing down his nervous system.

Get caught up with your hauling. Whatever your income is, save a percentage of it. Do not mistake us in thinking that we are preaching the old sermon of the savings bank, which is, save your pennies and the dollars will take care of themselves, for our friend Grizzly Pete of Frozen Dog, Idaho, says: "Save your pennies, the dollars will be blown in by your heirs."

No man gets rich through mere saving, but it is the training the man gets in saving the pennies that gives him a good idea of values of things and shows him the importance of having a reserve.

If the boss is extravagant in little things, the employe multiplies the extravagance.

If you are always catching up while you are an employe you will always be catching up while you are boss. If you are always saving and putting by a reserve while you are an employe, you will be doing the same thing when you are a boss. The principle is the same. It is merely a question of figures.

Do not take on financial responsibilities until you see your way clear to meet the responsibilities, and in addition to meeting them, see to it that you have made an allowance for good measure.

Catching up calls for double effort and double work.

Anger

In proportion as a man is wise, he controls his anger.

Centuries ago the following truth was written: "Whom the gods would destroy they first make angry," and in the same era there was also given us another truth: "A soft answer turneth away wrath."

A man's judgment gets twisted, his ground becomes insecure and his point of vantage weakens when he becomes angry.

The man who keeps calm when the other fellow gets angry has infinitely the best of the matter.

Let the other fellow fret and stew and get red in the face, but you keep calm and you will win the fight every time.

Control yourself, change the subject, and absent yourself when anger shows.

Cultivate poise, refrain from lowering yourself to the methods of the ignorant, which is anger. By keeping your temper when your adversary gets angry you thereby show your superiority, and your adversary instinctively feels you are a bigger man than he is.

A cool head is wonderful capital for an employer or an employe.

Don't mistake coolness and poise for submissiveness and servility. Don't let people impose on you and take advantage of your good nature.

State your position in cool, well-weighed words, and carry conviction with them by your manner.

It takes two to make a quarrel. Whenever anger is present, do not be one of the two.

Precedent

Precedent has caused many failures. We refuse to make a bold move and inaugurate a new system because we hate to break away from the methods established by successful predecessors.

We say "Let well enough alone." We forget that times change, and that conditions which made our competitors successful, may not now exist.

If you have the precedent habit it is an admission that you have not the brains to originate, and you are trying to take advantage of another's brains.

You remember the old fable of the lion and the jackass. The jackass was browsing on thistles in the desert. It took all his time to gather enough of the scanty vegetation to keep him alive. One day the jackass noticed the lion comfortably eating a lamb, whereupon he said "That's the scheme for me. I will do the same trick as Mr. Lion," and forth-with the jackass found a dead lion and covered himself with the lion's skin, hoping that with the lion's skin he would appear as a lion and thus be able to catch game in large portions, and relieve himself of this slow monotonous, hard work he had been used to. The jackass sallied forth, but he could not catch a lamb. He had copied the lion so far as physical appearances were concerned, but he did not have the brains of the lion, and he failed.

There are hundreds of wealthy business concerns today who are slowly dying from dry rot because they have not the nerve to break away from the precedent that built up their businesses. They let sentiment outweigh common sense. They maintain the same old lines and follow the same policy because that policy years before things made them successful.

Many manufacturers continue to advertise in publications which have long since lost their advertising value. These manufacturers have the habit, and on account of precedent they are afraid to break away. They do not recognize that since they started there are dozens of newer, brighter and better publications than the ones they are using.

Columbus, Marconi, Edison, Stevenson, Newton, Fulton, and hundreds of other originators would never have succeeded if they had followed precedent. They required strong courage to break away from accepted methods. Each of these men was told in so many words that the thing never had been done, and consequently could not be done.

Business men who throw aside precedent are more apt to succeed, for by throwing aside precedent they show they have originality instead of the ability to copy.

Financing

A financier and a general are much the same thing. The financier makes the dollars do the work at the best place, and the general does the same thing with his soldiers. The financier with plenty of money in the bank and the general with plenty of soldiers at his command are alike. They give the order and the thing is done, for they have the material to do the thing with. The difference between the good financier and the bad financier is like the difference between the good general and the bad one, the difference being that the good one makes a little go a long way, and gets the best results from the little under his command.

The cause of many failures is due to bad financing instead of bad business. The trouble is few business men know exactly "where they are at."

A detailed statement should be kept of all obligations. The business man should get along as far as possible without giving notes, and when he does give notes he should see to it that the notes are taken up when due.

The business man who overstocks shows he is a bad financier. The man who buys too much on possibilities makes a mistake.

As you go along this year you should make statistics of the receipts and expenses by the day, week, month and year. With these figures you can make up a budget of your receipts and expenses for the coming year with reasonable correctness.

Keep your resources well in hand. Buy often rather than buy in large quantities.

If you are owing money to the bank, have your plans arranged so that you can realize on your assets quickly.

The good general always plans his campaign to be ready for attack that may come through unexpected sources. The good financier is always ready for an attack on his finances.

The concerns from whom one buys may be prosperous. The bank with whom one deals may be flourishing, and yet without warning something happens and you are suddenly called upon to liquidate your indebtedness. You should be prepared for this sudden call.

Financing is an art, and you will never be a good financier unless you have had perplexing problems to solve. In order to solve problems you must have the pro and con, in other words, the details of your receipts and expenses. These figures should be put down plainly, with elaborate detail, if necessary, so you may count on your figures and make your plans accordingly. Preparing for emergencies is one of the first things the financier should understand.

Discontent

While in another part of this book we show that ambition is one of the things that makes success, yet it must not be forgotten that discontent is another great factor in bringing about success.

When the young man quits school he has life before him and has ambition to succeed. It is not particularly necessary that we find out what his ambition is to start him on the right path. Let the young man get started at any thing. If he is ambitious and has ability in him to manage a business he will get there finally.

He may get started in the wrong line and this will make him discontented. The discontent will cause him to try another tack, and so long as discontent makes him change he will finally get into the right line by the process of eliminating those callings which make him discontented.

Time after time we find in reading the stories of successful business men that they have floundered around in the beginning of their career from one business or calling to another. Discontented with each of them they changed and changed and changed until they finally struck the thing best suited to them, and all the changes they made in the past were distinctly beneficial because of the experience they obtained.

If it were not for discontent many of the leaders in the business world today would still be on the farm or clerking in a country store.

Keep busy, young man, do the first thing that comes handy. Change your job if you are discontented, for no one can do his best work if his heart is not in it. When discontent causes you to change frequently you may be sure that some day you will strike your gait, and then ambition will fire you to stick at it.

When you get on the right track and are not discontented you have struck it right.

The Generalist

The chapter on "The Specialist" is almost inseparable from this chapter. One is the positive, the other the negative. What we have said about the specialist we could repeat by taking the opposite of the question for the generalist.

This one point, however, we wish to make clear, even at the risk of repetition. Do not be a generalist in business. If you divide your efforts your results will surely be divided. The business man who goes in many outside ventures will not get along as far in the matter of wealth as the man who does one thing well.

We hear about "The jack of all trades," but the aftermath of the jack of all trades is "master of none."

Only one concern in fifty succeeds in business, therefore it calls for your best efforts if you wish to succeed. It calls for a singleness of purpose.

If you make more money than is necessary in your business put out the money in some form of investment that will require little of your attention. Buy mortgages or real estate. Get stuff that you can put in the green box in the safety deposit vault and not have to worry about.

The stockbroker has a lot of unwritten history about the business man who divides his energies between his office and the ticker. The business man who is trying to make more progress than his competitor in business and at the same time trying to beat out the stock market is dividing his energies, and between the two occupations he is likely to fail. Be a generalist in pleasure and recreation, but not in business.

Our Aches and Pains

When we work hard with our body all day our backs ache and our muscles ache. This is all right, for Nature has given us sweet refreshing slumber to drive away the aches and pains so that on the morrow we are ready for the fray.

In proportion as we have endured these backaches and pains and are patient in our occupation, the aches will lessen until finally we have laid up a store of energy so that the aches will not bother us.

The backaches and muscle-aches and headaches we have, when they come from honest work performed for the benefit of those we love, are sweet aches and pains. They represent sacrifice, these aches and pains do, and sacrifice brings happiness. The only way to be truly happy is to do something for somebody, and doing something for somebody is making a sacrifice for somebody.

The aches and pains we have endured in performing labor for those we love is the best evidence of genuine sacrifice.

We gladly suffer when our efforts are appreciated, and when those for whom we work are grateful, but there is one pain that never lessens, and it is the pain that kills. That pain is a heartache, and the heartache comes from ingratitude.

After we have endured backaches and headaches for those we love and find the effort has not been appreciated, then comes the heartache, and that is the ache that kills.

Whenever anyone does something for you, your first concern should be to show appreciation.

Gratitude is one of the most priceless gems in nature's collection. There is nothing lower on the face of the earth than an ingrate and a snake's belly.

Dressing

Many persons look upon the good dresser, and think that good dressing is an evidence of success. In dressing, as in everything else, the extremes should be avoided. The man who is temperate has the right idea. A man must be temperate in dressing as in all other things.

We have all seen the solicitor and the business man who look like a fashion plate or tailor's model. Each day he appears with a different suit. He wears the latest ties, the latest shoes, and appears in the height of fashion. This extra dresser is a four-flusher, for he is trying to appear as something that he is not. Grizzly Pete says "It ain't what's on a man but what's in him that counts."

In proportion as a man's character or mental training is lacking, he often tries to make up for it in dress. With some it is a case of ninety per cent. dress and ten per cent. man, and with others ninety per cent. man and ten per cent. dress.

In trying to find a word of cheer for the good dresser, the writer vainly endeavored to recall some successful business man who had climbed the ladder step by step through a period of years, during which he was always dressed in the height of fashion. We recall to mind several extreme dressers who are possessed of millions, but these millions were the result of accident or inheritance rather than ability. We cannot remember any instance of a plodder who started in with nothing and made his millions who during the operation dressed in extremes.

We have an autographed photograph of Marshall Field, and we venture to say that there are fifty men in Field's store more expensively dressed than Marshall Field was at the time this picture was taken, shortly before his death. Not that Marshall Field was poorly dressed, but that he was dressed like a gentleman. A gentleman does not wear extreme collars, extreme neckties, extreme coats. Marshall Field's clothes fitted him well, the goods were of splendid quality, but of modest design. Marshall Field was ninety per cent. man and ten per cent. dress.

When a man recognizes he has not the ability to make a name for himself on account of his brains, he resorts to dress in order to give him distinction.

The ability to dress in the extreme of fashion is an advertisement to the world that dress is your specialty, and if you are a specialist in dress you will not be a specialist in business.

Declare Monthly Dividends

Make it a rule to declare dividends every month. We venture to say to the business man that you are meeting all your fixed charges, paying your rent and employes, paying for postage stamps, lights, taxes and all other fixed charges. When the Government put a two cent tax on your checks you paid that tax. You certainly can add one more fixed charge to your business, and that fixed charge should be a percentage of your cash receipts.

It is usually a difficult thing to draw your profits out of your business in a lump at the end of the year, but if you draw your profits out in monthly installments, you can do so without any burden.

The business man should figure what percentage of his cash receipts is profit, and this percentage should be deducted every month, less a little leeway to make the matter easier. Make the percentage a fixed charge and put this money away in a special account as a reserve fund if you do not wish to draw the dividends out of your business. If you have this reserve fund drawn out in monthly installments, you are ready for attack if your creditors call on you suddenly.

If you have a snug little sum in a separate bank as a reserve sufficient to withstand any attacks on your business, your step will be more elastic, you will have more confidence in yourself, you will have less worry than if you are keeping your nose to the grindstone and have no reserve.

There is some amount between a dollar a week and a thousand dollars a week which you can draw out of your business without affecting it. If you make this a fixed charge you will take care of it, and you will arrange your business and your purchases so that this fixed charge will be properly taken care of each month. You will trim your expenses a little closer, and your business will thus benefit by having this fixed charge.

Nearly every failure is due to sudden calls of creditors or refusal of the bank to extend further credit. This fact shows plainly the necessity of having a reserve fund.

Take your figures for several years back and find what percentage of the total receipts was profit. If, for instance, your business earned $9,000 and your total sales were $100,000, then 9% of your receipts represents profits. You can therefore declare a monthly dividend of 8%, and when Christmas comes you will have an extra dividend, being the accumulated 1% each month you did not draw out in dividends.

Debt

If it were not for debt most banks would go out of business, for banks live because debt is a recognized factor in business.

The plan of getting rich through saving is a very difficult and practically impossible road to wealth.

The man who is working himself out of debt puts in better effort and longer hours into his business than the man who does not owe a cent. Go in debt reasonably and carefully, and you can make money with other people's money.

Money has a fixed value in itself in the matter of earning capacity. This fixed value is 5% or 6% or 7% as the case may be. One who puts his money in securities gets his money which the cash earns without effort on his part. The hustler, however, can make 10%, 15% or 20% on the money, plus his hard work. Therefore there is an opportunity for a hustler to borrow money at 5% or 6%, and with that money and his energy earn 10% or 15%.

The active man can therefore pay 6% per annum for money, and use that money to discount monthly bills at from 2% to 5%.

The building and loan association, the installment firms and monthly payment real estate concerns show what people can accomplish who go into debt. Thousands of families now live in their own homes because they went into debt. Few of these families would have homes if they started in on the saving-the-money-first plan and bought for cash.

Don't go in too deeply. Calculate your earnings in business. Allow a wide margin for discount on your figures. Hard times and unlocked for reverses come, therefore you should play safe. Go into debt on a 25% or 50% basis of what you are reasonably sure you can pay.

Up to forty years of age a man is sowing and tilling, and after forty he reaps. The farmer goes into debt during the spring and summer, and reaps in the fall.

Very few of our great men had much money before they were forty years old. Up to forty is the debt period. Up to forty a man pays interest; after forty he collects interest.

Business calls for the hardest kind of work up to forty or fifty. After that time the man makes up in judgment and experience what he lacks in physical activity.

Work hard until you are forty. Go into debt and make the money you have borrowed earn money. After forty make money by investing your funds in sound securities, so you will run no risk of losing what you have worked so hard for during your younger days.

The average banker is over forty. The hustling business man who borrows is usually under forty. Nature gives the young man ambition, ability and willingness. Nature gives the middle aged man judgment, experience and conservatism.

Forty years will determine what is in a man. If he has the stuff in him to earn a competence at forty, he has usually acquired the judgment and experience to keep it after he is forty.

The man born with a golden spoon never knows what hard work is. He does not go into debt because he has plenty of money for his requirements. At forty he has not the experience of his brother who was born in an environment of hard work and little money. The law of compensation thus bestows a subsidy on the poor boy and a handicap on the rich one to even things up. The poor boy goes into debt and works hard; the rich one lets the money do the work for him.

There is no joy or happiness in the possession of things we have not worked for, so while we envy the rich who have never worked we should take satisfaction in the law of compensation which gives us a subsidy in the way of ability to work hard and earn money, so that later on we may enjoy the money better than our rich friend who has never worked for his money.

Don't go into debt on the wholesale plan, hoping to make a big coup. Don't try to be a millionaire. Don't set too big a mark. Have your ideal advancement, no matter how little that advancement is. If you go forward each week or each year you will find at forty or fifty that your substance piles up much faster than you imagine. From forty to fifty years of age most fortunes are made. From twenty to forty your efforts have been foundation work, and the foundation does not show up much above the ground. From forty to fifty you are building the superstructure, and when you commence building that your progress seems more rapid.

Healthy indebtedness is a great incentive to hard work and a material benefit in building character and gaming experience that in later years will be of untold value to you.

Brains—Birth—Boodle

One of the weaknesses of the human race is envy. No one is entirely free from envy, although the true philosopher who has studied himself and has things sized up correctly is nearly free from envy.

Human kind have three measures for gauging the other fellow. We measure the other fellow either by his knowledge—which is brains, by his pedigree—which is birth, or by the money he has accumulated—which is boodle. These three Bs are like three stars in the sky. The first star—Brains is usually the dimmest, but it is really the brightest star of all. Mankind is prone to look at the brighter stars of birth and boodle.

These three stars of Brains, Birth and Boodle, are three aristocracies. The first aristocracy has no less authority than that of the Almighty. The aristocracies of birth and boodle are sham counterfeits gotten up by man. They do not mean anything when put into the crucible and tested by fire.

The aristocracy of brains differs from the aristocracies of birth and boodle as the sun differs from the jack-o-lantern, or as the music of the soul differs from the bray of the burro, or as a pure woman's love differs from the stolen affections hashed up by the fourth husband.

Brains like air and water, are not always appreciated until we have analyzed and investigated thoroughly. The foolish man thinks champagne is the finest drink. The wise man knows water is the best drink, even though water costs nothing. The foolish man has for his ideal—money or birth. The wise man takes off his hat to brains.

The measure of a man is his brain and not his birth or his boodle. Thought, reason and knowledge are possible to the man who has a brain. No man can buy brains, and truly he is an aristocrat of the highest order who is blessed with a good brain.

Some people whose ancestors came over with the Pilgrim Fathers have a picture of the Mayflower in their homes and they seem to take a great deal of pride in the picture of the Mayflower. There seems to be a halo around the Mayflower. The descendants of the passengers of that ship look upon the picture of the Mayflower as a sort of seal or guarantee of the good qualities of their forefathers, and consequently, being direct descendants they take unto themselves a lot of credit for something in which they had no hand in the making.

The Mayflower was afterwards used as a slave ship, but our disciples of birth do not want to know about this. Some of the passengers in the Mayflower performed acts and violated laws and conducted themselves in such a manner that would cause people of these days to be put in jail for the same offenses. Some of these good ancestors of the present descendants of birth burned witches at the stake.

Time wipes out a lot of things, and this is probably as it should be, but certainly it is true that the world is progressing and the good man of today is probably better and broader than some of these glorious ancestors to whom so many take off their hats. Some of our forefathers in Europe were little less than pirates and buccaneers. Their descendants today knowing that they can make great claims with little fear of contradiction, extol the virtue of their forefathers and complacently take on a superior air. They have thought over the matter of birth so much that they really think they are superior beings.

Grizzly Pete of Frozen Dog, Idaho, doesn't take much stock in the aristocracy of birth. He says, "It ain't what's on a man and it ain't what his father was that counts. The only thing to judge a man by is what's in him and what kind of brains he has."

One thing about this glorious Western country of ours is that a man gets credit for and he is punished by his own individual acts. It doesn't make any difference how far back his pedigree runs, if he doesn't make good himself, people have no use for him.

The heritage of birth is mighty thin fabric and mighty weak material for a man to use in making a cloak of exclusiveness to put around him.

We anticipate that some of our readers will take exception to our attitude on the matter of birth. We wish to be plainly understood that the matter of good birth and good ancestors is a good thing to have. The writer has a pedigree that would be his passport into the aristocracy of birth if he chose to belong to that lodge. Your good ancestors is no handicap. It is a credit to you, but mark this down well: You, yourself, are entitled to no credit for any acts of your ancestors. Your measure is and should be taken for what your own net worth is.

The aristocracy of boodle is the slimmest aristocracy of all. Yet there are more people who try to get into that lodge than any other. The possession of the dollar seems to be the ambition of everyone, and usually the first thing we try to find out about a man is "how much is he worth?" The thinker, however, knows that the possession of money doesn't make a man any better than his neighbor who has no money—their morals and their acts being even.

Brains. That's the true aristocracy. The professor in college who has spent a lifetime in study and has devoted his talents to uplifting mankind is an aristocrat. He may be getting two or three thousand dollars a year, while his brother with lesser knowledge is getting ten times that much in another vocation. The aristocracy of brains always has been, is now and ever will be the enduring aristocracy. Even those who belong to the aristocracies of birth and boodle find they are sham counterfeits and many of them turn to study and to good impulses hoping they may get into the lodge of the aristocracy of brain.

In business the aristocracy of birth or the aristocracy of boodle is a decided handicap. They make the individual think he is superior and he is above doing things which seem to him trivial, because he thinks he is a superior being. The man with brains, however, digs as well as climbs. Without brains, business would go to the dogs, for if business were conducted by men of birth and boodle without brains, you can easily see that the whole fabric would fall to pieces.

Backbone and Wishbone

In proportion as a man's backbone weakens his wishbone seems to develop.

The ten dollar a week man spends his time saying: "I wish I had the luck other people have." He says: "I wish I had this place, or I wish I had that job." He is ever wishing.

Things in our body, whether muscle or bone, develop by usage, and if we use the wishbone all the time it will develop into huge proportions. On the other hand if we develop our backbone and use it frequently, we may not have cause to use the wishbone so much.

Brace up. Stand erect. Strengthen your backbone and, with it, your jaw bone.

Say "I will" instead of "I wish." The world bestows her prizes on men with backbone and the blanks on those who use their wishbone.

Do Good

Doing good is planting seed, the harvest may not show at present but in the future you are going to reap it.

A man is paid back precisely in the same coin he pays out. If he plants weeds or mean impulses the harvest will be weeds and mean impulses. If he plants seed of good deeds he will harvest good deeds.

Centuries ago it was said "Cast your bread upon the waters and it will return to you many-fold."

The man who is doing good as he goes along, who is lending help, kindly counsel and encouragement will find the world is a pretty good place to live in after all. As he journeys along through life he will find the good he has done in the past has flourished and returned to him in greatly increased proportions, like the bread cast upon the waters.

It is not only the good one actually gets for the good, he has done, but it is the profit that comes in the way of happiness he gets for his actions. The true way to obtain happiness is to do something for somebody. You get back out of the general exchequer of good in the world full payment for the good you have done, plus a profit of happiness which comes from the very doing of good.

The Get-Away

After you have driven the nail home make your get-away.

Many a solicitor has lost his prestige because, after having accomplished his point, he hung on.

It is quite an art to know when to make the get-away. Study your customer carefully, and when you have made your point clear and your proposition is presented to him in the best possible manner, then get away.

The bore is a bore because he does not know how to get away. The solicitor is always welcome if it is known he is not a hanger-on, and that he gets in and gets out quickly.

Double Equipment

For the employe there is nothing better to possess than double equipment, by which we mean the ability to do two things well.

From the employer's standpoint nothing will stand his business in such good stead as to have his employes doubly equipped.

In the printing business, for instance, the old time printer knew how to set type, lock up forms and to run a press.

Nowadays we seldom find a printer in the broad sense of the word.

In the big printing establishment we find the various branches of the printing trade have employes who are specialists at one thing. In the printing trade the craftsman is either a compositor a proof-reader, a make-up man, a pressman or a binder.

The employe who can set type and also run a press is a decided advantage to the employer. The writer knows a certain publishing house whose every employe is doubly equipped. The rule of the proprietor is that every job or branch of the business must have more than one person competent to run it, and that every person must know how to do two things.

Double equipment on the part of the employe gives the employer great resources.

When sickness, accident or other causes prevent the employe from filling his accustomed place, then the proprietor can call on others who have the double equipment, to fill in the gap.

The employe who is following a particular line in the establishment should acquaint himself with some other branch of the business or some other trade, if he is a craftsman.

The employe who is doubly equipped is decidedly at an advantage over the employe who knows but one thing.

Initiative

Initiative is simply the willingness and ability on the part of an employe to do things that are not simply routine, to do things he is not told to do, to look for opportunities to help the boss or to improve the business wherever possible.

The employe who has no initiative in his make up is going around a circle and when you go around a circle you don't go forward. There is no one thing outside of honesty, ability and hard work that will help the employe to go forward like initiative.

In every great business there are many opportunities for the employe to do things he is not told to do and when an employe gets the initiative habit he is not long in attracting the attention of the boss.

Look over the work you are doing, study the matter carefully, figure out some plan whereby the value of the work you are doing will be increased.

Find a chance to lessen the expense in your department.

Put into practice some idea that will increase the receipts.

Acquaint yourself with the operations of other employes in similar work. Wherever you find a plan better than yours, take advantage of it.

Keep your eyes wide open and you will find many opportunities for doing things you are not told to do.

Every employe should carry out to the letter the directions given him by the boss and in addition to this he should have initiative, which is doing things the boss did not tell him.

It is the plus or initiative in a man's make-up that helps him to the front.

Night Work

It is always a question among experienced business men whether night work and Sunday work help the game of business.

Of course there are occasions when a job must be finished or work completed within a specified time and if you are behind with your hauling, it is necessary to turn all your resources into a singleness of purpose to get the thing done.

The trouble is, however, that many business men figure on this night work as part of the regular scheme and in this they overdo the matter.

The law of compensation says that a man is good for just so much work and if he spreads the work over into longer hours the intrinsic value of each hour is lessened.

A man who habitually takes work to his home to finish and counts upon these extra hours, will soon find the value of his work decreases.

We should all remember that we should work while we work and play while we play.

Work hard during your business hours, conserve your energies, but outside of business hours, let play, study and recreation occupy your time.

If you go home from business at night and forget the things you have been doing in the day and use your time for the things in life outside of business, the next day, when you go to your office, you can make things fly.

It is proverbial that the busy man is the one to go to if you wish things done promptly.

Those of us who were born and reared in the country know a familiar type that is to be found in every country town.

He may be a carpenter or blacksmith, or may run a repair shop of some kind. We find him going to the post office in the middle of the day to get his mail. We frequently find him in the back part of the country store playing checkers. At other times he is watching a horse trade. Again he is arguing politics. This man does not get in over four or five hours' simon pure hard work in a day.

You take a job to this man and it will drag days and weeks. You become impatient at the delay. You get after the man and his answer is that he has not the time.

It is practically a truism that those who offer the excuse that they have not the time are really the ones that have the time.

Some of our friends treat us shabbily in the matter of correspondence and when you get a letter from one of them, he says: "Excuse me for not writing sooner, but I really have been so busy that I have not had the time to write."

As a matter of fact it takes five or ten minutes to write a letter and the person who pleads for forgiveness through lack of time has wasted a hundred times the minutes necessary to write a letter.

The busy man, accepts his duty as a matter of course, a ranges his correspondence and work in systematic order and goes at the thing, hammer and tongs, and gets the thing done.

Night work is usually evidence that the man does not do his work properly in the day time and he is like our friend in the country who wastes time in the day and tries to make up for it by night work.

The thing to do is to work hard in the day time and rest at night.

Obedience

Several years ago, our friend Elbert Hubbard wrote a little sermonette entitled "Carrying the Message to Garcia." The story was simply this: President McKinley called an orderly and gave him a letter and said: "Deliver this letter to General Garcia."

The employe did not stand around and ask a lot of fool questions about the trains and things. He put on his hat and duster and he delivered the letter to Garcia. These facts were stretched out in many words and made a little booklet. That booklet reached the sale of more than a million copies.

It seemed to make a hit with business men throughout the country. A certain railroad bought and gave a copy to every employe. Business men followed the example. The great sale of the book and the wide-spread interest it created would seem to indicate that carrying the message to Garcia was an unusual thing and so remarkable that it attracted attention.

As a matter of fact the whole theme of the story was simple obedience.

There are thousands of institutions in this country who have employes who will carry the message to Garcia.

Richard Harding Davis, you remember, was dining with friends in London. The discussion was along the lines of obedience and the like.

On a wager he called a messenger boy, gave him a letter addressed to his fiancee in Chicago, told the messenger boy to deliver the letter to the lady and bring back an answer. That fifteen year old boy carried the message to Garcia, or in other words to Mr. Davis' sweetheart.

The Colonel of a regiment has under him about twelve hundred men. Directly under him are his majors, and then come the captains, lieutenants, sergeants, corporals and privates. The first rule in the army is obedience of orders without question.

If obedience were subject to question on the part of the subordinates, the colonel could win no battles.

When your superior gives an order, the thing to do is to carry it out. If the order is wrong you will not be to blame, but your superior will suffer.

There are times, of course, when an order is given that is manifestly impracticable and initiative on the part of the employe might save trouble.

On the other hand, an executive would be greatly handicapped if his orders were subject to interpretation and analysis by his subordinates.

The executive may give an order and in the giving have in his own mind the relation of this order to some other order he has given in an entirely different department and upon the proper execution of all the orders given through the various departments depends the ultimate success of his plan.

The thing for the employe to do is to obey orders willingly, quickly and to the letter.

The employe is not blamed when he does his duty.

It is a source of great satisfaction to the boss to know he has dependable employes and that when he gives an order the thing is done so far as further effort on his part is concerned.

Pay Day

We have all tried all sorts of plans regarding pay day, but the plan most satisfactory to all concerned is to pay each Tuesday or each Monday for the previous week. If the nature of your business is such that Monday is an unusually busy day, then Tuesday should be your pay day.

Monday is usually called blue Monday, because the employes blot out some of the sunshine on Sunday by thinking of the hard week's work ahead of them. Much of the blueness is driven away, however, if in looking forward they know that Monday or Tuesday they will get their pay checks.

The old fashioned habit of paying off Saturday nights is a bad one, especially if most of the employes are men.

Many men are weak and it is difficult for them to pass a lot of saloons on Saturday night without the money in their pockets burning a hole.

The Saturday pay day may mean that a percentage of your employes will not show up on Monday morning. Many men will go on a spree on Saturday night on the theory that they can rest up on Sunday, who would not think of going on a spree on Monday night or Tuesday night, for it would interfere with the work next day.

The writer does not know of a single concern that has adopted this Monday or Tuesday pay day plan and practiced it for a reasonable time without finding it works admirably. Try it in your business and you will not go back to the Saturday pay day.

Saving

We will not indulge in the proverbs handed out by the savings bank in the matter of saving. We are not pessimistic when we say that no man ever became wealthy through the savings bank plan of putting away a certain amount each week. We will say, however, that there is no better training for the employe than this one thing of saving. Saving a part of your weekly income and putting it away, if carried on for a number of years becomes a habit and it means that you will keep your expenses within your income. It is the saving habit that makes the benefit, for later on when you are in business the habit stands you in good stead and teaches you the value of having a reserve.

By all means, put away a certain amount each week. If it is not a dollar, put away fifty cents. If that is too much, put away half of it, or even ten cents a week.

Have some amount as a fixed charge in your operations and put this amount in the savings bank. Later on your balance will grow and you will have much satisfaction in watching its development to better proportions.

Habitual saving makes you careful in the things you do. It teaches you the relationship between principal and interest. It shows you that when you buy something useless and pay ten dollars for it that it is costing you interest each year to maintain it.

The man who does not save is pretty sure to live beyond his means and some day trouble or affliction will come and he will be out of a job and then he appreciates the difference between the butterfly and the bee.

When you haven't anything to fall back upon, the world is a mighty blue place. When you have money in the bank it is a mighty good place to live in.

Waiting For Success

It takes a good poker-player to know when to lay down his hand.

It's a wise business-man who knows when to quit a forlorn hope.

It's all right to build up a business. It is all wrong to play a losing game in business for a succession of years in the hopes of ultimate success.

As years go by the business man is establishing matters on a firmer and more solid foundation. Sales generally increase; the volume of the business gradually grows greater. This fact is responsible for many business men continuing their business at a loss, lured on by the hope of final success. It's all right to build a reputation and to be patient, but when the odds are against you and by all the changes you make and all the brains and ingenuity you put into your business, you cannot turn it into a profitable basis, then get out of that business and start something new.

It's all right to build, provided that as you go along you are making a living profit, but dogged determination to play a losing game year after year is not to a man's credit.

Every man has some particular channel in which his talents will fit and produce good results. If your business goes along year after year at a loss, it is evident that your talents are not in the right channel.

The great thing in business is that it shall respond quickly and show signs of life right away. If it does not, then the business is wrong.

The shores of the great ocean of business are strewn with wrecks which have been dashed to pieces on the rocks sailing for that false beacon light, "keep everlastingly at it brings success."

This saying is true, providing you are making expenses and some profit as you go along, but to keep everlastingly at it when your business shows a loss means failure.

The thing that lures many on is the increased sales. Meanwhile, the expenses are increasing proportionately, and if these two lines are always parallel, there is no hope of your making a success. Better quit before you get too deep in the hole and have a lot of "dead horses" to pay for.

It's all right to have ambition, tenacity and patience in business and to look forward to the far future as crowning success of your efforts, but it's all wrong unless you are paying expenses and making a living while doing these things.

Our Sons

The noblest and most important work we have to do is the training and teaching of the coming generation.

The successful business man has no more difficult problem to solve than what he will do with his son.

It is a fact that the greatest successes in the business world today are those men who had to start in the battle early, and fight their way to the front.

The successful business man usually tries to arrange matters so that his son will not require to go through the hard working school of experience he himself attended, and in this the business man rather goes to the other extreme in that he tries to make things easy for his boy.

As the twig is bent so the tree is inclined. The young mind is plastic and capable of receiving impressions, and we know that the impressions made in our youth are lasting all our days.

The problem in the country is not so difficult, for there are so many things to do about the home that the young country boy usually has plenty of chores and duties to perform.

Occupation is a decided blessing and a present benefit to a boy.

People in the cities have all creature comforts about the homes, transportation facilities are ample, the homes are heated by steam, stores are in abundance, people buy from day to day, and every little convenience is at hand to keep the scheme of living going along smoothly.

Because the city boy is surrounded with schools and the comforts of home he has much time on his hands. The boy is active, and if his activity is not turned on useful things, it will be turned on useless things. The young boy goes to the grammar school, and the daylight hours, outside of school hours, are devoted to play. This is right and as it should be, but when the boy gets along to twelve or fourteen years of age, the parents should arrange for him some little duties, some regular task to perform. The youngster will get accustomed to this, and it is decidedly beneficial. As the boy enters the high school he finds his hours shorter and his leisure hours longer.

The high school period is a most important one in the boy's life, and the father should see to it that the high school boy is occupied for several hours each day, either in his own place of business or in some other establishment.

There is no way of teaching a boy the value of money like having him work for money.

Arrange to pay your boy so much an hour for the duties he performs. Have his occupation regular, talk with him about what he has done during the day, be a companion to the boy, and soon you will notice that he evinces interest in the things he is doing, and as time passes, ambition is fired in his breast, and when the time comes for him to enter the threshold of business he has been prepared for the work.

It is strange that while we parents realize the importance of education, we pay so little attention to the boy while he is going to school. We should keep in touch with the boy's teachers and with the boy himself, taking an interest in his studies. The business man as a rule drifts apart from his son during his younger years.

There is nothing that will help the boy so much as being a companion to him, being interested with him in the things he does, whether work or study. Fathers and sons should be comrades.

A close companionship between father and son is not only a great satisfaction and source of happiness to each of them, but is decidedly beneficial to both.

By all means have some regular occupation for your boy while he is going to school. Keep in close touch with him. Explain to him the things he does not understand. Show him the great possibilities ahead of him if he does right, and the impossibility for him to succeed if he does wrong.

Pull

The young man who is expecting to get a fat job through pull is working on a false basis. The young man whose objective is to get a snap shows he has not ambition, and surely this young man will occupy inferior positions as long as he gets a job through pull.

There is a legitimate pull in business, and that is activity and ability. Don't look for snaps. Snaps are merely traps. Men are not paid for snaps, but for snap.

The average young man just out of college looks for a job through the pull of his father or some relation, and in this he is making a great error. The best way to get a job is to get it without pull through your own energy and aggressiveness.

The best jobs are obtained through push and not pull.

The City Hall and Government buildings all have the word "pull" on the front door, and in direct contrast with this you will notice the front doors of the successful business institutions are marked "push."

Gossip

It is surprising to see the extent to which gossip is carried on among business men. The funny papers always refer to women and the members of the sewing societies as gossips of the first class, but if the gossip going around business circles could be tabulated, we are sure the sewing society would have the joke on us.

It is a footless thing to spend valuable time in idle gossip, for the gossip is seldom a successful business man.

Gossip takes hold of some men to such an extent that most of their waking hours are spent in finding out something to tell to someone else, and thus leaves but little time for business.

Bribes

Many business men seem to think that bribes are efficient helps. It is not so. The moment you bribe a person you acknowledge your dishonesty by paying for his dishonesty, and you may be sure that the bribe habit will grow; the demands of the men accepting the bribe will grow to alarming proportions. For every dollar you make by bribing someone, you are losing ten dollars in other ways, especially in your own self respect and satisfaction.

The moment you give a bribe you are under obligations, and some day or other the facts will be brought out and you will suffer the consequences of your own weakness.

Underhand, clandestine information you get is no more than dishonesty on your part. You can get better information and accomplish your purpose more surely by going direct to a competitor, stating your case plainly, and announcing your abhorrence of underhand methods. Your competitor will appreciate you more for your fairness, and he will go out of his way to give you information when you have shown you are square.

Stenographers

Few young men realize the advantage of learning stenography. We all know the young man who writes shorthand comes in touch with the boss at once, and while acting as amanuensis or secretary is getting a schooling that money could not buy. He is going through and becoming familiar with business as it actually exists.

He sees the decisions made by his employer, and he unconsciously absorbs methods which would be almost impossible for him to learn were it not for his proximity to the boss.

Shorthand is decidedly beneficial, first—because it is a good training for the mind; second—it is a help all through one's life. It enables him to take down memoranda and keep notes of verbal transactions; it enables him to get in the private office, and to be in the middle of the nerve centers of business.

Some of the greatest men in this country were shorthand writers. The stenographer who is alert soon gets to the center of the business; he soon has responsibilities given him by the boss, and is in direct line for promotion.

Hypochondriacs

Here is a type we run across every day in business. We see the apparently well man taking out a pill box or a bottle of medicine as he sits down to lunch. We ask him what is the matter, and he proceeds to tell us about his bodily ills and infirmities.

Many men seem to take a keen delight in having something the matter with them. They go to a physician, though often the disease is practically mental.

You can't get health out of a glass bottle. The man who is taking medicine all the time is going at things wrong end to. If his stomach is out of whack he should change his method of living rather than to try to cure his dyspepsia with stuff that comes in a bottle.

The man who needs a tonic before he can eat a lunch had better take plenty of air and exercise than to take poisonous drugs into his system.

If you are a smoker and find you have no appetite for lunch, give up cigars in the forenoon, and you will notice an immediate difference when you sit down to the noonday meal.

The hypochondriac imagines he has things the matter with him, and he becomes confirmed in his belief, he finds that so long as he lives he has something the matter with him. He no sooner gets cured of one than something else attacks him. There is no medicine like air and exercise and occupation. The man who gives in to trifling ailments is in a sad plight. He is never happy unless he is sick. He is unreasonable, and he is the last one to appreciate what can be done by a man who cures himself through the mental processes.

We all know that we can take a perfectly well man and pre-arrange to have a dozen of his friends on a given day greet him with some remark about his ill appearance. That man will be sick before the tenth man accosts him.

Politics

Politics is a losing game. Every man owes it to himself and to his family and to his country to take an interest in politics to the extent of getting out to the primaries and voting for the right man, and help to get good men in office. But when a man carries politics to extremes or mixes it with his business, his business is sure to suffer.

There are two kinds of politics—the honest kind and the grafting kind. The honest politician gets very slight remuneration for the time and energy he spends, and the grafting politician sooner or later winds up in the soup through his dishonest practices.

There is no greater danger to business than to have the proprietor spend much of his time in politics. The upright business man will not descend to the things practised by the dishonest politician, and the sharp business man who has no compunctions on this score will make a loss in his business.

The law of compensation surely comes in here, for in proportion as a man plays politics his business is bound to suffer.

Profanity

Twenty-five years ago profanity was found on every side. Today you find it only among laborers. Business men won't allow profanity.

Swearing goes with lying. The truthful man can look you in the eye and chisel out his words and you know he means it.

The liar gets angry and swears, and he is a bluff.

Truth doesn't need curse words to make it stick.

Some great men swear and many small men swear. Usually, however, the truly great man doesn't swear.

Men who think, men who study and analyze, seldom swear.

Swear words are usually used as fillers in sentences. Some men have limited knowledge of adjectives so they resort to swearing.

Mark this when you hear a man firing a volley of profanity in rapid succession—You lose respect for that man!

Profanity is an easier habit to acquire and harder to give up than its distant relative, slang.

Slang has its value for it has taken place of much profanity.

Slang and profanity, and logic and thought don't mix well together. The more profanity, the less brains in your make-up. Profanity is a hold-back.

System

System is all right so long as it lessens labor. Generally system is complex and increases fixed charges.

The system of copying every letter is a waste of time. Not once in a thousand cases do you require to refer to a letter.

Have fixed rules and prices and you won't have to refer to letters.

When you do copy a letter copy it on the back of the letter you are answering. Use a carbon sheet.

Have Simplicity your rule instead of System.

System has tangled many institutions.

Beware of system that makes more work.

Don't clutter up your office with a lot of useless data and wagon loads of old letters and records.

Rule of Gold

Centuries ago Confucius was walking through the woods soliloquizing and analyzing and sizing up things in solitude. While thus engaged he was waylaid by two Chinese peasants. These men had heard of Confucius' philosophy, but they could not make much out of it, for Confucius used words beyond their limited understanding. These men, with raised clubs, halted Confucius and said to him: "Our minds are small. We do not understand the things you say. Tell us how to live. Make your story short or we will slay you. We can only remember as much as you can tell in a moment. Therefore, stand on one foot and tell us quickly what we are to do. We can only remember what you can tell while standing on one foot."

Confucius stood on one foot and said: "Sing, fat, bong, lung, looy," which, being interpreted, means "what you would like others to do to you, do to them."

This is the golden rule which has been handed down through centuries. It has been alloyed and simulated. It has been attacked, but, like all pure gold, it has endured forever. There is no line of action we can suggest or anything that will prove more valuable to the young man or old man through life than the golden rule.

The golden rule is not theoretical, but a wholly practical help, and so in closing this series of talks with you, the writer feels that the essence of all the logic, good advice and philosophy may be summed up in the following:

"Do unto others as you would have others do unto you."

In saying good-bye we suggest that you particularly remember the key to knowledge, which is O.R.B., and which means Observe, Reflect and Benefit, and the practice of the following: Work, Horse Sense and Golden Rule.